WHAT OTHERS THINK ABOUT
THE FIVE KEYS

"Having been involved in Continuous Improvement/Process Improvement for more than 30 years both "in the trenches" and as a senior management consultant around the world I'm often cautious when I see new books in this field. Typically, I expect the same-old-same-old restated in new terms or words. This book is just the opposite. Dave and Jim have taken years of experience, research and analysis and pared it down into five concepts (the Five Keys) that makes it easier to take common sense and put it into common practice.

Written for the practitioner, the curious and the novice The Five Keys is a well-crafted book that flows extremely well. The authors use real world experience to bridge the gap between theory and implementation. If you're new to the field, just getting caught up, or thinking about taking the plunge with your organization I'd strongly suggest that you take the time to read this book. Absorb what it says and then put it to work. Your chances for success will definitely be enhanced."

George Byrne
Managing Partner - Nictom Consulting Group
Executive Director of Operations Excellence (United States & India) - Deloitte Services, LLP

"Real world strategies for organizational change. This book is a must read for every leader committed to sustainable improvements."

Brian DeWyngaert, Chief of Staff,
American Federation of Government Employees

"Hats off to Jim and David McNeil for this practical and engaging contribution to the body of literature on process improvement. Having partnered with Jim for over two decades on a variety of strategic planning, visioning and leadership development initiatives, I know firsthand that the lessons shared in The Five Keys can support any organization committed to sustainable process improvement. In an era where "disruption" has become a constant consideration, this book is a welcome resource for any leader looking to gain a competitive edge."

Sukari Pinnock-Fitts, MSOD, PCC
Shiftwork, LLC
Professor, Human Resources Masters Program,
Georgetown University, School of Continuing Studies

"Throughout my career I have been involved with numerous continuous improvement initiatives. I have had the opportunity to work with both Jim and David McNeil and experienced their passion for Improvement and their understanding of techniques to unleash it within others. While many programs focus on lean principals, those technical skills are only a start. Jim and David have a way of teaching that sustainment only happens when you address the human element, "the culture". This book covers the many facets which need to be understood to achieve transformation and be successful long term."

"I would consider it a "must read for leaders looking to start a continuous improvement initiative or for those asking: are we getting the results we expect?"

Joseph W. Simkulak, CPA, CPIM
Chief Financial Officer, Intermetro Industries

"This book is a fun read. It explores a little history, and then develops the elements, of continuous improvement, bringing it down to five basic keys. It includes a pair of case examples which help highlight and explain the five keys. I encourage individuals who are interested in establishing a sustainable basis of continuous improvement within their enterprise, to read through this book and be enlightened by it. You're bound to get a perspective which will stretch you and which is new and interesting. Enjoy the read."

Dr. Gerhard Plenert, PhD
Former Missionary, Philippines San Pablo Mission,
Former Director of Executive Education, The Shingo Prize
Institute, Utah State University

"Jim and David get to the core of Improvement with this book! They have taken their many years of experience and really hit the mark on what it takes to succeed with Improvement efforts in any organization. Through their use of examples and clear to understand principles, you too can achieve real sustainable improvements by applying this book to your Improvement journey! I would highly recommend the Five Keys for all leaders at any level in an organization to read this treasure and apply its many gems to your own Improvement efforts!"

Jeff Watson, Sr. Engineer
and Improvement/ISO 9001 Leader

THE

FIVE

KEYS

TO CONTINUOUS IMPROVEMENT

Unlock the Potential in Your Organization

David & Jim McNeil

SECOND EDITION

The Five Keys to Continuous Improvement: Unlock the Potential in Your Organization

Limit of Liability/Disclaimer of Warranties

ISBN: 978-1-7364053-5-2

I0135351

ACKNOWLEDGMENTS

We acknowledge with enormous gratitude those who have shared with us their knowledge, expertise, and passion for bringing change to organizations and individuals around the world. It is in their spirit that we share what we have learned with you. We thank:

Our many clients, who, over the past 30 years, trusted us to work with them in creating organizations of "world-class" stature.

Our colleagues and partners at Competitive Dynamics International who encouraged us to persevere in writing this book and for over a decade generously shared their experiences and expertise with us.

Allen Sievertsen, Jack Mihalko, Jillian Kriger, George Byrne, Thom McNeil, and Dan McNeil read early drafts of this work and provided honest and thoughtful advice. Their contributions are noteworthy and truly appreciated.

Doug Williams is our editor and his counsel, critiques and attention to details have guided us in writing and re-writing this book. His contributions cannot be overstated.

David Zeolla has assumed the role of editor for this Second Edition. His experience and knowledge guided us successfully throughout the process.

Bobbie R. Deen, Graphic Designer, provided terrific graphics that are posted throughout.

Cheryl Jones has continually supported our efforts by updating our work, correcting our errors and keeping the writing process moving.

Finally, we especially wish to thank our family members who were supportive and encouraged us to stick to it. Family tended to the many obligations and chores of daily life while we typed away in seclusion. We could not have completed our work without them. Extra-Special thanks to Pauline and Beth.

FOREWORD

BY DREW MARK BUTLER

I have spent my entire life in manufacturing and operations, starting as machine operator and advancing to my current role as Vice President of Operations. The one common theme during my entire career was a drive to make things better and not being satisfied with the status quo. There are a few instances in my life where I can think back to moments that changed the direction of my career, graduating from college while working full time, working with Mr. Shimbo from Shingijutsu, becoming a Shingo Examiner and meeting Jim and David McNeil.

There are not many people you come across in your life who truly make a difference in the world. I can honestly say that Jim and David McNeil have made a difference in mine. I am excited for you to read this book so that you can get to know them like I do, and experience the genuineness, warmth and incredible knowledge that they possess. Then I challenge you to experiment with their thoughts and ideas to better your world. When people tell me how hard it is to change their organizations, I always use examples of Jim's time as a UAW president to illustrate change in a difficult environment.

The format of this book is excellent, each chapter explores different topics that are critical to implementing change. They are discussed in an order that will maximize the results for your organization. For example, in chapter one they lay the foundation of continuous improvement and give a brief history of it. I especially liked this chapter because it discusses the inter-connectedness of systems and departments and how it is critical for practitioners to understand to create that Culture of Continuous Improvement, every day, everywhere! In other words, you cannot change one without affecting the many. Chapter one has great thoughts on how to implement specific behaviors and a culture that will support the tools and systems of Continuous Improvement.

An important section of the book is Chapter Two, where they discuss the Five Keys. Their example of how two identical sites got two different results on their Continuous Improvement journey while basically using the same implementation plan, systems and tools is fascinating. The 5 keys that they discuss are ideas that I often refer to when people ask me "Where do I begin with change? How do I create a culture of Continuous Improvement?"

If you are like me, you will find yourself reading this book repeatedly and using it as a reference in your journey. As I was reading this book it brought back many great memories of time spent with Jim and David and their teachings. One of the best memories I have with them, is working with them to engage the workforce at my site. We wanted everyone to enjoy their jobs and feel that they are part of an important purpose; the process was invigorating. This book has captured the "magic" that impacted my world.

Drew Mark Butler,

Vice President of Operations, Signs.com
Shingo Examiner and Certified Shingo Facilitator
Salt Lake City, Utah
November 2020

DEDICATION

This book is **written for the tens of thousands of individuals charged with leading continuous improvement efforts for their business, organization, or association**. This legion is made up of leaders ranging from CEOs to front-line employees. Their responsibilities range from developing and implementing strategic plans to pursuing incremental improvement opportunities. No matter where you may fall on this broad spectrum — CEO, the front line, or the hundreds of positions in between — your future and that of your organization are directly impacted by how successful you and your colleagues will ultimately be.

To ensure we are all speaking the same parlance, we use the phrase continuous improvement or CI throughout the book as an umbrella term for long-standing and ongoing improvement initiatives such as: Process Improvement, Operational Excellence, Total Quality Management, Lean Production, Toyota Production System (TPS), Performance Improvement, Process Excellence, Kaizen, Quality Assurance, Strategic Effectiveness and other titles for ongoing programs dedicated to improving an organization's functions and processes.

We differentiate between improvement programs, adopted and titled by various organizations, from the vast array of improvement "tools" such as: TQM, A3, Six Sigma, Five S (5S), FIFO, Heijunka, PDCA, Standard Work, Kanban, Value Stream Mapping (VSM), Hoshin Kanri, Visual Controls, etc.

ABOUT THE AUTHORS

Jim McNeil, left and David McNeil

DAVID MCNEIL is the Director of Continuous Improvement, North America at Competitive Dynamics International (CDI), a consulting company with clients, past and present, in over 80 countries and more than 3,000 worksites. CDI is dedicated to implementing, sustaining, and growing continuous improvement initiatives world-wide. For over a decade, he has guided dozens of organizations in their quest for continuous improvement, employee engagement, and intentional culture change.

JIM MCNEIL is an organizational change specialist bringing four decades of hands-on experience to the work. He has provided direction and support to organizations in the United States and Europe from the boardroom to the front lines. In his early days, he served as a union leader for 25 years in the United Auto Workers, successfully bringing changes to a very complex environment. His clients include: corporations, nonprofits, governmental agencies, and trade unions. Industry experience includes: service, manufacturing, health care, pharmaceutical, telecom and advanced technologies.

CONTENTS

INTRODUCTION

"Everybody has a plan until they get punched in the mouth."

–Mike Tyson

Heavyweight boxer Mike Tyson's famous quote captures the stark reality of life: that regardless of planning and preparation, things change and change quickly. The relevance of this quote and life lesson was forever driven home as the Covid-19 Virus began to reap havoc across the globe. It was that "punch in the mouth" the world had not anticipated nor adequately planned for. As the disease spread from Wuhan across China, this epidemic rapidly spiraled into a global pandemic, the likes not seen in over 100 years. Hundreds of thousands of lives have been lost to this "punch" and those numbers continue to mount. You had to wonder how many lives would have been saved and resulting economic chaos avoided if health agencies and governments had been able to quickly react. They simply failed.

If ever there was a moment validating the benefits of developing and maintaining a culture that is versatile, innovative, and engaged, it was revealed during the most desperate days following the Covid-19 outbreak. Companies as far afield as the hospital care and medical equipment communities to the manufacturers of autos, apparel, vacuum cleaners, air-bags, electronics, and dozens of other specialties rapidly transformed their manufacturing capabilities to save lives.

These diverse enterprises, almost overnight, shifted production from their traditional product lines to urgently needed ventilators, face shields, reusable gowns, respirators, face masks, and test kits. Their swift response helped protect health care workers and save the lives of the tens-of-thousands who were sick and dying.

The Covid-19 global pandemic, like other global crises, brought about structural changes to organizations of all types. We see dramatic examples of how education, travel, shopping, recreation, medical treatment, food production, dining, and even houses of worship have adapted – some better than others. We can expect, as we emerge from this calamity, other industries and organizations will be similarly challenged to create their new normal.

Some consider the ability to rapidly pivot, innovate and capitalize on turmoil a miracle! However, those of us in the continuous improvement field see these capabilities as tangible benefits associated with a participative and engaged workforce. As demonstrated by the many of organizations that quickly responded to the call, those groups are equally prepared for business challenges that confront them.

Time will inevitably heal the deep wounds inflicted by the Covid-19 Virus yet the need for preparedness will always be with us. The ability to pivot, adapt, and prosper, regardless of the challenges and obstacles faced, is vital to all successful organizations and their members.

The Process-improvement Puzzle

Organizations around the world have launched, in one form or another, hundreds of thousands of improvement initiatives during the last 25 years. These efforts were conceived with the best of intentions, and staffed with capable people to lead the charge. Unfortunately for many, their efforts fell short of the desired bottom-line impact and many improvements were simply not sustainable.

Over the past two decades, we have researched and analyzed the reasons why some improvement efforts generate great results and why others fall short. **Through trial and error, we have explored differing strategies, designs, methods, and tools, and over time, zeroed in on those specific aspects of continuous improvement we found most critical for sustainable success.**

Why We Wrote This Book: 'Solving the Puzzle'

Over the course of a decade, while working with a client at two "sister sites" located some 100 miles apart, we experienced very different results. These manufacturing facilities were located in similar communities, produced the exact same product, with the exact same equipment and technology. They reported to the same corporate hierarchy, relied on the same internal support networks, and had the same suppliers and customers.

Given the similarities of these two sites, you would expect similar results – not exact, but similar. If only that were true… One site became the company's North American model for continuous improvement, while the other site struggled with poor or mediocre performance, higher internal safety violations, and greater turnover. How could that be? Why were results so dissimilar? Why was it a joy to work at one site and a constant uphill challenge at the other? What were we missing?

As consultants for both locations, we continually pondered this dilemma, sharing our conundrum with others in our international consulting group. Collectively, our 20-year old international consulting team has clients in 80 countries around the globe. Together we have launched continuous improvement initiatives at over 3,000 different client sites. Each member in our group has experienced the joy and pride associated with great successes and suffered disappointment in lackluster results. We were determined to discover the reasons why!

The more we worked through this real-time challenge, the more we recognized the need to solve this puzzle. In doing so, we might discover the linchpin for many organizations embarking upon the improvement journey. We had to find the answer.

We decided to zero-in on identifying and standardizing the most critical aspects that buttress our most successful process-improvement initiatives. Regardless of the specific improvement an organization embarks upon, we found that combining certain behavioral science principles with *five strategic components*, which we refer to as *the five keys*, can transform a complacent culture into one committed to continuous improvement. In this book, we present our learnings to you in a way that enables you to implement them at your worksite.

SECTION 1

ROOTS

In our decades of leading improvement efforts, we've come
across some well-known and some lesser-known concepts
and models that we have found to be both foundational and
requisite in our work with a variety of clients.

As continuous improvement leaders, it is vital to adopt a
"continuous learning mindset." This approach to your work
provides you and your organization with unlimited opportunities
to gather knowledge from your experience, formal and informal

educational opportunities, training sessions, interaction with others in the field, as well as your work colleagues.

Each new improvement initiative creates the opportunity to learn and grow as the individuals, the environment, the improvement challenge and the work itself are all somewhat different.

Obviously, you can't know something until you learn it, but where do you go and whom do you talk to in order to gain this understanding? We believe this book can help.

The Roots section presents several short segments containing a collection of history, research, experiential learnings and behavioral science teachings that have enabled us to jump start improvement efforts and assist organizations laying their own grounds for continuous improvement. They include:

▶   The Chronology of Continuous Improvement

▶   Business Systems

▶   The Formula for Change

▶   The Diffusion of Innovation

▶   Culture

CONTINUOUS IMPROVEMENT

Continuous Improvement: A philosophy and business approach devoted to the continual improvement of processes, products, and services. Efforts focus on changes for the better, both incremental and breakthrough.

"Continuous improvement is not about the things you do well — that's work. Continuous improvement is about removing the things that get in the way of your work. The headaches, the things that slow you down, that's what continuous improvement is all about."

Bruce Hamilton, Director Emeritus Shingo Institute

Early Years	1920 - 1980	1985 - 2015
Eli Whitney c. 1790 Idea of interchangeable parts	Walter Shewhart c. 1920 Statistical Control – Control Charts "Total Quality Management"	Bill Smith c. 1986 Motorola Engineer, "Six Sigma"
Frederick Taylor C. 1890 Time & Motion "Scientific Management		Allied Signal & Maytag c. 1990
Henry Ford c. 1910 Moving Assembly Line"	Joseph M. Juran c. 1930 "Quality Control Handbook"	Independently developed systems Combining concepts "Lean Six Sigma"
Frank Gilbreth c. 1911 Process Charts – Motion Studies	W. Edwards Deming c. 1950 "PDCA Cycle", "14 points"	Womack, Jones & Roos c. 1990 "The machine that Changed the World" –
Lilian Gilbreth c. 1915 Industrial Psychologist Production / Efficiency	Sakichi Toyoda c. 1960 Founder of Toyota Industries, "Just-In-Time Production"	Lean Thinking. TBM Consulting Group c. 2010 "Lean Sigma"
	Taichi Ohno c. 1970 "Toyota Production System"	

The Evolution of Process Improvement

The concept of implementing improvements has always been an instinctive factor in human nature and part of our human story since the cavemen. It is common sense to find ways to make work easier and improvements sustainable.

In the chart above, you can see "game-changers" in the evolution of process improvement dating back to the 18th century. These "breakthroughs" occurred rarely, yet dramatically reshaped the industries where they originated. But it was in the post-World War II era that the notion of "continuous improvement" began to enter the mainstream lexicon and migrated from inventors and theorists to a more mainstream audience involving workers on the front lines.

Continuous Improvement Gains Traction

Continuous Improvement (CI) or Continual Improvement Processes (CIP) accelerated markedly in Japan after World War II. Japanese industries were decimated during the war and the United States provided experts to assist with the rebuild. One of several experts, sent by the U.S., was Dr. W. Edwards Deming an American statistician, originally sent to Japan to assist with census work. During the World War II, Deming was a member of the Emergency Technical Committee, a group charged with developing statistical methods for quality control of materials and products, and taught Statistical Process Control (SPC) to manufacturers engaged in the United States' war materials production. Based on his wartime experience of improving quality and reducing waste, he was recruited to assist the Japanese in their manufacturing rebuilding efforts.

Deming introduced Japanese industrial leaders to his brand of statistical process control, quality control, and the "Shewhart Cycle" which evolved into the Plan-Do-Study-Act process. Deming, was certainly not the sole inspiration in helping the Japanese rebuild their industries; however, Deming was unrelenting in his focus on improving quality, eliminating waste, and weeding out non-value-added steps in the manufacturing process. He urged companies to focus on streamlining their processes by engaging their frontline workers in these improvement efforts. The approach was known in Japan as "kaizen," translated literally as "improvement."

During the 1950s, Japanese products had a global reputation for low costs and poor quality, and were derided by many Westerners as "junk." But in order for Japan to ever recover economically as a nation, their leaders knew that their success was directly tied to their ability to export. And, in order to export successfully, they knew their products must reflect high quality and be produced cost-effectively.

Let the Good Times Roll

While Japan was in the midst of its industrial revolution, American industry paid little attention — and for good reasons. During the war and thereafter, America became a manufacturing juggernaut. Throughout the war, mass production methods had been fine-tuned, and as the war ended, American consumers were hungry for new everything. Between 1945 and 1949, Americans purchased 20 million refrigerators, 21.4 million cars and 5.5 million stoves. In the 1950s, televisions and auto sales skyrocketed.[1]

Practically every item that American industry built would be sold, and ravenous consumer spending would continue during the 1950s and 60s. Due to the lack of rivals to American industry, manufacturers were not interested in process improvement or quality controls, and opted instead for greater output.

---

1   The American Experience." The Rise of American
      Consumerism". Library of Congress.

Quality and cost were non- issues: American industries could sell anything they produced and increased production costs would be passed directly on to insatiable consumers. In this environment, it was not surprising that American industry was not seeking improvements and instead followed the approach of "if it ain't broke, don't fix it."

Conversely, throughout the 1960s and 1970s, Japanese manufacturers distinguished themselves in the production of high-quality textiles, consumer electronics, cameras, watches, appliances, and automobiles. Products from Japan, once considered "cheap" or of "poor quality," had now become market leaders.

Sony and Panasonic began to dominate the electronics industry, while Toyota and Honda were manufacturing and exporting high-quality, smaller fuel-efficient vehicles. From the ashes of the war, Japan had been rebuilt and become the world's second largest economy, second only to the US, from 1968-2010.[2]

The Oil Crises of 1973 & 1979

The 1973 oil crisis began in October 1973 when the members of the Organization of Arab Petroleum Exporting Countries (OPEC) proclaimed an oil embargo. The embargo was targeted at nations perceived to be supporting Israel during the Yom Kippur War. The nations initially targeted were Canada, Japan, the Netherlands, the United Kingdom and the United States, later extended to Portugal, Rhodesia and South Africa.

By the end of the embargo in March 1974, the price of oil had risen nearly 400%, from US $3 per barrel to nearly $12 globally; US prices were significantly higher. The embargo caused an oil

---

2   Web-Japan n.d.

THE FIVE KEYS TO CONTINUOUS IMPROVEMENT

crisis, or "shock," with many short- and long-term effects on global politics and the global economy.[3]

This "first oil shock" was followed by a second. In 1979 a decrease in oil output occurred in the wake of the Iranian revolution. Although supplies only decreased by 4%, widespread panic resulted causing crude oil prices to spike at nearly $40 dollars a barrel. Then in 1980, the outbreak of war between Iran and Iraq resulted in severe production shortages triggering recessions in the United States and other countries. Oil prices did not subside to pre-crisis levels until the mid-1980s.[4]

Global Paradigm Shift

These "oil shocks" appeared to trigger a paradigm shift throughout the world and especially in America, Western Europe, and Canada. No longer was cheap fuel a given, and as a result, consumer tastes began to forever change. Car buyers now demanded fuel efficiency and higher quality. For North American auto and steel producers specializing in the high-volume production of large, fuel thirsty vehicles, this change represented a cataclysmic shift in demand.

While tumultuous shifts in manufacturing and technology had occurred in the past (i.e., textiles, electronics, apparel mills, mining), it seems that this upending of US auto and steel industries, considered the bellwether of American manufacturing, signaled a tipping point extending far beyond these two industries.

---

3   CBC News. Archived from the original on June 9 n.d.). (Milestones 1969-1976 Oil Embargo n.d.)

4   Vessela Chakarova and others. 2013. Federal Reserve History. November 22. Accessed 2020. https://www.federalreservehistory.org/essays/oil_shock_of_1978_79

11 | DAVID AND JIM McNEIL

Before long, other commercial sectors began experiencing similar customer demands for higher quality and lower prices. As trade barriers fell away, increased competition from around the world forced businesses in a variety of commercial sectors to reinvent how products would be designed and manufactured.

Consumers had awakened to new brands and marketplaces. Enter the advent of Global Competition.

The New Reality

During the ensuing decades, global competitive pressures on businesses and industries to continually improve increased steadily. As technology, process, design, and services became easily transportable, unlikely competitors continued to sprout.

Some businesses found they were no longer anchored in their country of origin, and began relocating to take advantage of low wages, the absence of labor and environmental regulations, and overall cheaper production costs outside the US. Companies of all types now took careful note of their global competition.

And throughout the world, many businesses wisely invested in revitalizing their manufacturing facilities while introducing Japanese inspired "lean" work practices to their worksites

So, it is here that we find ourselves today *in an unrelenting contest to produce quality goods and services faster and more cost-effectively than our competitors. It is here that continuous improvement is invaluable.*

Continuous Improvement Becomes a Way of Life

Given the ever-changing dynamics of global competition, today's business leaders should feel no less desperate nor committed than those leaders in Japan after the war. To continually improve is not an option, but a necessity. To remain a viable organization today, you must continually get better. "Good enough" will not sustain most organizations going forward. Today, it is demanded that all organizations continually improve. Failing to do so is a risk to the survival of the institution.

Continuous Improvement is an indispensable methodology essential for all business types to effectively compete. CI is a cornerstone of a successful business strategy in every sector and every nation. Deming provided us with a successful business philosophy that has withstood the test of time and that can be applied in a hospital, bank, or paper company, in *Fortune* 500 companies or nonprofit organizations, in the private or public sector.

The Benefits of Continuous Improvement

The positive impact of establishing a continuous improvement culture within your organization can be immense. Sustainable leaps in bottom line profitability, volume increases, improved quality, reduced costs, enhanced safety, employee sponsored innovations and engagement are some of many gains cited by our clients over the past 25 years.

The Philosophy

Continuous Improvement or Kaizen is a philosophy – a way of thinking – a workplace culture. This approach continually seeks to identify and implement small incremental changes for the better. It recognizes that the people best-positioned to do this are those on the front lines — the people who work with the process daily and can recognize these opportunities. Of course, major process improvements are not discouraged, but these breakthroughs occur infrequently and often at a high cost. By contrast, small improvements over time can and do lead to significant gains for the organization. (see the graphs below)

Features of Kaizen – Continuous Improvement

▶ A focus on many small improvements over time.

▶ Many small improvements often out-perform infrequent major breakthroughs.

▶ Small improvements typically require lower capital expenditures.

▶ Small improvements can be rapidly implemented.

▶ Improvement ideas frequently come from the front lines – the people closest to the work.

▶ Small changes are likely to encounter less resistance.

▶ Employees and front-line management take greater ownership – people support what they help create.

The Essence of Continuous Improvement

While many programs for continual improvement are available, the essence of CI remains much the same as those principles articulated by Deming nearly 7 decades ago:

"Improve constantly and forever every process for planning, production and service"

— Dr. W. Edwards Deming

This is done by:

▶ Developing sound leadership.

▶ Engaging all employees in your efforts.

▶ Aligning goals throughout.

▶ Demanding accountability.

▶ Providing adequate resources and training where needed.

In 1951, the Deming Prize was established by the Japanese Scientists and Engineers Association – JUSE, in tribute to Deming, recognizing individuals and businesses for their contribution to the field of Total Quality Management. In 1960, Deming was awarded the Second Order Medal of the Sacred Treasure by Japanese Emperor Hirohito honoring achievements in quality.

David Salsburg wrote: [5]

"Ford Motor Company was one of the first American corporations to seek help from Deming. In 1981, Ford's sales were falling. Between 1979 and 1982, Ford had incurred $3 billion in losses. Ford's newly appointed Corporate Quality Director, Larry Moore, was charged with recruiting Deming to help jump-start a quality movement at Ford. Deming questioned the company's culture and the way its managers operated. To Ford's surprise, Deming talked not about quality, but about management. He told Ford that management actions were responsible for 85% of all problems in developing better cars. In 1986, Ford came out with a profitable line of cars, the Taurus-Sable line. In a letter to Autoweek, Donald Petersen, then Ford chairman, said, 'We are moving toward building a quality culture at Ford and the many changes that have been taking place here have their roots directly in Deming's teachings.' By 1986, Ford had become the most profitable American auto company. For the first time since the 1920s, its earnings had exceeded those of

---

5   David Salsburg . Course Hero - Texas A&M University.
     https://www.coursehero.com/file/prdt5a/David-Salsburg-wrote-
     He-was-known-for-his-kindness-to-and-consideration-for/

archrival General Motors (GM). Ford had come to lead the American automobile industry in improvements. Ford's following years' earnings confirmed that its success was not a fluke, for its earnings continued to exceed GM and Chrysler's."

The Power of Continuous Improvement and Incremental Change

One of the biggest challenges faced by today's executive boards and senior management is the need for tangible and immediate results. The pursuit of quarterly profits that is driven by financial markets and shareholders often causes executives to focus on the short term and commit their strained and limited resources to the "program of the day" or "flavor of the month." The quest to achieve immediate outcomes rather than longer-term sustainable results can actually diminish an organization's overall return on investment when contrasted with deliberate and methodical improvement efforts.

A major fix, such as reengineering a process, typically is a one-time change that requires a significant investment in time, money, and resources. All too often, resources are taken away from daily activities in order to address a major problem that is hurting operations, stakeholders, or customers. The fix will achieve immediate results, which are often not sustainable, and the organization finds itself addressing the same issue a few years later.

Now what if an organization could achieve even better results that are sustainable over the long-term without requiring resources to be pulled from their jobs? A continuous improvement culture, one where employees view their everyday job as improvement facilitators, can do just that. In the graphs below, developed by George Byrne, it is obvious how the compounding effects of a continuous improvement culture outweighs the one-time benefits of reengineering a single process.

Continuous improvement of a process normally addresses production output or effectiveness. But what if we applied that same principle to cost reduction or the efficiency of a process? Once again, as depicted in the second graphic below, continuous cost reductions over time, as opposed to a one-time reengineering reduction, are both greater and more sustainable in the long run. In the hyper-competitive world in which most organizations operate today, it is important to create a culture that values and drives continuous improvement. Even as organization leaders seek to improve operations, costs, production, and other facets critical to business success, managers must remember that their competitors are not standing still. Staying ahead requires not just vision and planning. It requires a means by which the entire organization is aligned and getting better each and every day. Continuous improvement is a major enabler to that end.

Any one of the four facets of Operational Excellence can be achieved through a single 100% increase or through incremental improvements over time.

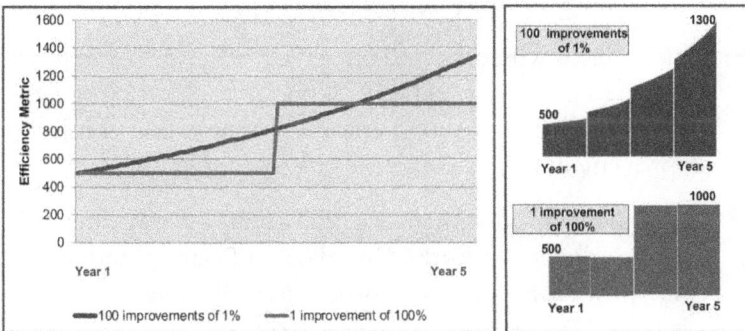

In theory, numerous 1% improvements over time have a compounding effect and hence are more effective than a sole 100% improvement

What could this concept mean for costs?

Said another way, what if we viewed the facet of cost reduction the same way?

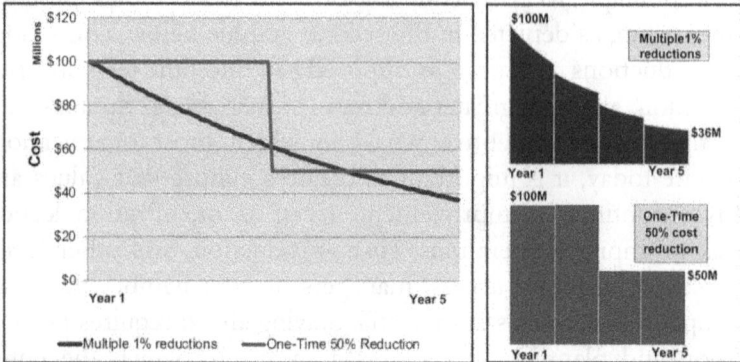

—Multiple 1% reductions   —One-Time 50% Reduction

Instead of a one-time significant reduction in costs, the firm would undergo continuous cost reductions with better long-term sustainable results.

🖐 TAKEAWAYS

▶ This reality is where we find ourselves today; in an unrelenting contest to produce goods and services faster and more cost-effectively than your competitors. It is here that continuous improvement is invaluable.

▶ Continuous Improvement is a philosophy – a way of thinking — a workplace culture. "Improve constantly and forever every process for planning, production and service"

▶ Staying ahead requires not just vision and planning. It requires a means by which the entire organization is aligned and getting better each and every day. Continuous Improvement is a major enabler to that end.

BUSINESS SYSTEMS

Business system: A system designed to connect all of an organization's intricate parts and interrelated steps to work together for the achievement of the business strategy. Effective business systems should unify the problem-solving and decision-making of the organization.

"If you're too busy to build good systems, then you'll always be too busy."

— **Brian Logue**[6]

Exploring Systems

To make lasting change in your organization, it is essential to understand the inter-connectedness of the various internal functions. Just as a tossed pebble creates ripples across the entire pond, so too does change in one segment of your worksite impact many others.

A typical business organization consists of several major functions or departments. In manufacturing, for example, these functions are often labeled as: sales and marketing, manufacturing and production, research and development, finance and accounting,

---

6   Rudi Jansen. "If You Are Too Busy To Build Good Systems You'll Always Be Too Busy." February, 2019.
https://www.rudijansen.com/too-busy-to-build-good-systems/

and human resources. Additionally, there are other indirect functions or services that are vital to the organization, such as suppliers and product-distribution networks.

While each department and function are somewhat independent, they perform as a whole, providing the goods or services to their customers. Each area is linked together and depends on each other in order to meet the goals of the enterprise. If one of these functions is inefficient, dysfunctional, or implements a change, the impact is felt throughout the entire organization. Using our manufacturing example, if the production process is beset with a quality problem, that problem negatively impacts the entire organization – from front to back.

Understanding this interdependence and how it impacts your continuous improvement efforts is vital. Even subtle changes in method, materials, measurement, machines, people, and even the environment are likely to impact some or all of the other functions within the organization.

Silo Mentality

The Business Dictionary defines The Silo Mentality as a mindset present when certain departments or sectors do not wish to share information with others in the same company. This type of mentality will reduce efficiency in the overall operation, reduce morale, and may contribute to the demise of a productive company culture.[7]

In a 2013 *Forbes* article, the authors describe what they believe to be the cause of this dysfunction: "The silo mindset does not appear accidentally nor is it a coincidence that most organizations struggle with interdepartmental turf wars. When we take a deeper

---

7   The Business Directory.
     http://www.businessdictionary.com/definition/silo-
     mentality.html

look at the root cause of these issues, we find that more often than not silos are the result of a conflicted leadership team." [8]

Our experience is slightly different but the result is the same. We have found that the silo effect often resides in the notion that knowledge is power and by sharing my information I lose power and others gain — the classic win-lose scenario. Also, it can be risky for managers to tell the boss or share with others insight or information they deem detrimental and would rather not hear. No one wishes to be the bearer of bad news.

Regardless of the reasons, the net result is inefficiency, incomplete decision making, distrust and team dysfunction.

What to do: be mindful that, to some degree, this malady afflicts many organizations – if not most! As a CI leader, you can construct conversations that lower participants' inhibitions about sharing completely their views and advice. In order to do this, you must make it safe, from both the standpoint of sharing good as well as bad information.

Buried Alive

The interconnectedness of departments and functions can and often does make the work of change more difficult. Take the following example from our work with one of our large international clients: the billing department's management team concluded that they were buried under needless paperwork from past transactions. The area where these old paper transactions were stored was floor to ceiling in their main billing office. Twenty plus years of paper transactions were held, even though these

---

8   Gleeson Rozo. "The Silo Mentality: How to Break Down the Barriers." *Forbes*. October, 2020.
     https://www.forbes.com/sites/brentgleeson/2013/10/02/the-silo-mentality-how-to-break-down-the-barriers/#49414b318c7e

same transactions were stored digitally on hard drives. Each transaction continued to be both digital and on paper forms.

Management agreed to free the business of this time and resource-draining record collection process – a great continuous improvement idea!

Implementing this change was dependent on the interrelationship between departments. The site leader first approached the HR manager for their assistance, who took their improvement idea to the legal department for advice.

And there it died. Month after month of no response from Legal finally came to an end when six frustrating months later, Legal finally acknowledged that no one was willing to make a decision about when and if paper transactions could be discarded. This seemingly simple, time- and effort-saving improvement suggestion died on the vine.

If only situations like this were uncommon; but unfortunately, they are not. In retrospect, if we, as consultants, had advised the billing department management to include the other departments in the development of this project, we would have either gained their support and advice or learned early on that disposal of old records was not permissible. By doing so, all parties would have avoided the frustration and disappointment that added a dose of cynicism to the mix.

Like Tossing a Pebble in a Pond

The last week of each month would always wreak havoc across one of our client's systems. As the month's end approached, company sales representatives mounted an all-out blitz, generating a slew of last-minute orders that were required to be built and delivered before the month's end. This flurry each month was driven by the desire to meet corporate sales forecasts and monthly sales incentives.

Typically, discounts and other customer benefits were provided to secure these new orders. Our client, a company well known in their industry for Five-Star customer service, then needed to produce and ship these orders all within one week!

What happened next demonstrates the interconnectedness of this company's business structure. The orders, now considered RUSH, moved from the Sales Group to the Planning Office. The products produced by this client were quite complex, requiring precision in both raw-material sizing and construction in order to meet customer-specific requirements and rigid safety standards.

The Planning Department now had to revise the production plans at two manufacturing sites located many miles apart. Plant A produced the base materials required for the finished product (these varied depending on the order) and Plant B had to assemble and test the new products. In order to meet the new schedule, production changes at both factories were necessary. The changes, which were very disruptive and time-consuming, frustrated both plant management and their employees, creating added work and huge losses in productivity.

Once the product was produced, each item was then subjected to extensive safety and quality checks. As these requirements were met, the product would then be prepared for shipping. Here again, logistics struggled to secure overnight transport resulting in high drama and additional costs.

After the products were delivered, the Finance and Accounting group now needed to expedite their financing and billings in order to meet the deadline.

This true scenario demonstrates how one function — "Sales" — set in motion a cascade of actions that impacted each and every department across the entire system.

Collaboration and Communications

"Systems thinking" (a holistic approach to understanding how various independent parts influence one another within the whole – think ecosystem with air, water, plants and animals working together to survive) makes clear the need for collaboration. As you embark on your CI initiative, it is wise to ensure that all the various functions of your organization are aware, or part of your planning and implementation. Including representatives from your various site functions (i.e., sales and marketing, operations, research and development, finance and accounting, and human resources, etc.) on a steering group is one way to build support for your initiatives while minimizing adverse reactions to changes you may advocate. At a minimum, communicating effectively and regularly with all functions and eliciting feedback from them can pay big dividends as your efforts gain momentum.

TAKEAWAYS

▶ Each function or department within your organization will likely be impacted by continuous improvement initiatives.

▶ Build support for your program, and the impact that may result, by including other business function leaders in your project discussions.

▶ Communicate continually with all business functions citing progress and potential impact.

FORMULA FOR CHANGE

"It is not the strongest or the most intelligent who will survive but those who can best manage change.

— **Charles Darwin**

As a Continuous Improvement leader, it is important to have an overall understanding of how to establish the conditions where change has the opportunity to occur.

We wish to share with you a simple and effective model that will enable you to set in motion a change process allowing your efforts to take hold. *The DVF model is one that has guided our work for decades.* It was developed from the work of organizational theorist Richard Beckhard[9] and refined in the 1980s by Kathie Dannemiller,[10] one of the most respected organizational development consultants of her era. Dannemiller's version explains what it takes to bring about real change in an organization or in an individual. It begins with a given: "we all resist change to some extent." This holds true in our personal lives as well as our working lives. Our resistance is rooted in our survival instinct and our desire to avoid unknown risks. While it's not a prerequisite to uncover the origins of each person's resistance to change, what is important is to know how to overcome this natural instinct.

---

9   Carrie Foster. Organization Development. September, 2012. http://organisationdevelopment.org/the-theorists-richard-beckhard/

10   Dannemiller-Tyson Associates . *Whole-Scale Change - Unleashing the Magic in Organizations.* (San Francisco: Berrett-Koehler , 2000.)

THE CHANGE FORMULA
D x V x F > R

Dissatisfaction	Vision	First Steps	Resistance
with the current	of a positive	in the direction	to change
situation	possibility	of the vision	

Dissatisfaction x Vision x First Steps > "Resistance"

$$D \times V \times F > R$$

Dissatisfaction with the Current Situation

The first step is for each individual and the organization as a whole to understand and share a common *dissatisfaction* with the way things are right now — the "D." "D" describes *why we must change*, the reason for us to do anything differently.

The D (dissatisfaction) must be honest and compelling. It must be explained and be understood throughout your organization. If there is no *dissatisfaction*, no compelling reason why this continuous improvement effort is vital, then it joins the dozens of other programs competing for your organization's limited resources. Just another flavor of the month.

$$D \times V \times F > R$$

Vision of a Positive Possibility

The second step is to establish a *common vision*. That *vision* describes a future state the organization seeks to achieve. It is your end state, your target. This vision "V" must be clear, articulated and understood throughout your organization. It is a picture of the future, that motivates and is important to achieve.

According to John Kotter in his book *Leading Change*,[11] a vision should serve three purposes:

1. Clarifying the general direction for change, it simplifies hundreds or thousands of more detailed decisions.

2. It motivates people to take action in the right direction even if the initial steps are personally painful.

3. It helps coordinate the actions of different people across the organization.

$$D \times V \times F > R$$

First Steps in the direction of the vision

The third step refers to *"F" first steps* – those significant system-wide concrete actions that will begin to move the organization toward the vision. *First Steps* lifts the cloud of uncertainty by announcing **how** the organization will move ahead. It also signals

---

11   John Kotter. *Leading Change*. (Brighton, MA: Harvard Business Review Press.) 2012.

that this change effort is more than just talk and words on a wall – it's about action!

$$D \times V \times F > R$$

Resistance to Change

Resistance is normal, natural, and to be anticipated. Both individually and as members of an organization, we humans have an innate desire to resist change. In the 1920s, H.P. Lovecraft said: "The oldest and strongest emotion of mankind is fear, and the oldest and strongest kind of fear is fear of the unknown."[12]

This is *why if any of these three elements — "D" "V" or "F" — is zero or hollow, the drive for change cannot overcome the natural forces of resistance "R" that exist within any individual or organization.* Your efforts will fail.

More Than a Model

The DVF model is a great deal more than simply a formula for change. It is, in fact, a vehicle that enables the necessary *transition in thinking* to occur. When you help your organization to combine D, V and F, colleagues can begin to glimpse a larger picture and different perspectives. As this happens, the system, as a whole, transitions and so do your colleagues as individuals.

Now the organization, (individually and as a whole) are seeing a more complete picture of what lies ahead. The fear of the unknown has been addressed and the vision now points the way forward.

---

12 H.P. Lovecraft. *Supernatural Horror in Literature*. (Mineola, NY: Dover Publishing, 1973).

This model offers a tested protocol for CI leaders to follow.

It is the cornerstone for your continuous improvement efforts.

TAKEAWAYS

▶ The D x V x F > R "formula for change" applies to individuals and organizations.

▶ This formula is a sequential chain, therefore if any of the three elements Dissatisfaction, Vision or First Steps is zero or hollow, the drive for change is unlikely to overcome the Resistance – failure becomes likely.

▶ The DVF model enables the necessary transition in thinking to occur.

The Formula for Change template is available for download at www.thefivekeys.org

DIFFUSION OF INNOVATIONS

"When an idea reaches critical mass there is no stopping the shift its presence will induce."

— Marianne Williamson[13]

Anyone with experience introducing continuous improvement initiatives will acknowledge that the adoption of a change effort required more time and patience than originally anticipated. We have learned that it is important to plan accordingly and not attempt to compel compliance – it doesn't work. Even small changes in organizations require time for people to assess and accept all that those changes entail and the impact on themselves personally.

For employees to truly support and get behind a change effort, a **critical mass** must be convinced. Until then, the majority will not join and come on board. When a new program, new technology, or improvement initiative is introduced into a work system, even if many think the idea is a good one, most employees are reluctant to show support until they are persuaded that their colleagues also are getting behind it. Change will be slow until a critical mass is reached; then, a snowball effect often takes place.

The graph below, based on the theory developed by E.M. Rogers in 1962,[14] demonstrates the adoption sequence for a new concept, idea, behavior, innovation, or product among individuals and organizations. The graph tells us that, regardless of the beneficial aspects of an innovation, its adoption does not happen

---

13   Marianne Williamson, American author

14   E.M. Rogers. *Diffusion of Innovations* . (New York: Free Press. 1962).

simultaneously among all those impacted. Some will adopt an innovation faster than others and some, perhaps never.

As a CI leader, it is important to understand that the adoption of innovations does not distinguish between executives, managers, supervisors, and the front-line employees. In each of these employee groups, you likely will find colleagues who fall into all five adopter categories. Just *because someone holds a managerial role, you cannot assume that they will endorse the change initiative.* Managers, like their front-line colleagues, will assess the likely impact of the initiative for themselves and what that means to them now and in the future.

Adopter Categories

The research by Rogers, in his book *Diffusion of Innovations*, reveals that distinct characteristics define the adopter categories: Innovators, Early Adopters, Early Majority, Late Majority and Laggards. The chart below can help you identify the additional information that each adopter category may require to respond positively to the innovation.[15]

---

15   Everett M. Rogers, Diffusion of Innovations (1st ed.). (New York: Free Press of Glencoe, 1962.)

THE FIVE KEYS TO CONTINUOUS IMPROVEMENT

Adopter Categories	Who they are	What they need to see / hear
Innovators 2.5%	**Risk Takers.** Those willing to lead the charge.	Not much. These folks are on board.
Early Adopters 13.5%	**Opinion leaders.** Comfortable with innovation and implementing new ideas. Recognize the change as needed.	No need to convince them. Share specifics and details. How we intend to launch. Measures of success, etc.
Early Majority 34%	**Thinkers.** Likes to see evidence that innovation meets expectations. Readily adopt new ideas.	Want to see evidence that new initiative will work at your worksite. Share progress, gains and successes.
Late Majority 34%	**Skeptics.** Will come aboard after the majority have adopted the innovation.	Looking for proof that initiative is supported by their colleagues, or evidence that the innovation has been successful.
Laggards 16%	**Traditionalists.** Will commit only after the idea had become mainstream.	Don't write these people off. Provide statistics and positive results. Make clear the impact if the initiative is unsuccessful.

Barbara Wejnert. "Integrating models of diffusion of innovations: a conceptual framework". Annual Review of Sociology. 297–326.

👆 TAKEAWAYS

▶ Even small changes in organizations take time as people assess what the change entails and the impact on them personally.

▶ Just because someone holds a managerial role, do not take for granted that they will endorse the change initiative.

▶ Three critical factors likely to impact the rate at which critical mass accelerates:

- How quickly and enthusiastically "leaders" embrace the change.

- The complexity of the change and ease of implementation.

- Clear and immediate benefits.

CULTURE

Culture: Culture is that blend of shared values, history, traditions and all those unwritten rules, behaviors, habits, attitudes, and practices that work colleagues share and ultimately drive the results and performance of the organization.
"It's the way we do things around here" - the living personality and character of an organization.

"Culture eats strategy for breakfast"

— attributed to Peter Drucker[16]

What's The Culture Like In Your Organization?

Forget the words on the wall! The organization's Vision, Mission, Values. If you really wish to explore the "real culture" of an organization, ask several employees privately and confidentially a few of these questions:

▶ "What's it like to work here?"

▶ "What's really important?"

▶ "How do people act when no one is watching?"

---

16   Peter Drucker. *The Essential Drucker*. (New York: Harper, 2001).

▶ "What do I need to know to get along?"

▶ "Who gets promoted and for what?"

▶ "Would you recommend working here to a family member?"

What you will hear and quickly learn is the actual culture being described by those who are living it! Now, contrast those descriptions from the employees with the words on the wall. Do they match or even resemble each other? In some organizations the answer is, "yes absolutely," but in far too many, you might more easily compare night and day.

Having worked with dozens of different organizations developing and articulating their vision, mission and values, and subsequently their strategic plans, we are acutely aware of how executive leaders struggle to capture just the right words and phrases that they hope will inspire and guide their organizations for years to come. These statements should drive improvements and guide decision-making throughout the organization – that is, if the vison and the culture are aligned. This is why the culture in an organization is so important: **If an organization's culture is incompatible with its vision and strategy, the likely result is failure to achieve its goals!**

Take the following example:

Vision: To be recognized as the premier industry leader providing our customers with unsurpassed products and services by 20YY.

Strategy: Our vision will become reality through an empowered workforce with self-directed teams in each department, and all employees directly engaged in solving problems and continuous improvement activities.

Now, in our chart below, compare the vision and strategy to the organization's current culture. If the characteristics of their work culture is traditional (below left) and the vision and strategy call for empowered employees focused on continuous improvement (below right), *what odds would you give this organization for realizing their vision?* Unless the culture changes, there is little likelihood that the organization will realize its vision.

Traditional Work Culture	CI Work Culture
Authoritative / Bureaucratic	Entrepreneurial, innovative, informal
Individualistic	Teams and teamwork
Limited communications – need to know basis	Open / transparent – sharing good news and bad
Little connection to customers	Customer focused
Supervisors solve problems	Team members solve problems together
Accountable only for my work	Accountable for team's performance
Focus on daily requirements	Common Goals and Measures
Risk adverse	Risk tolerant

Unless the culture changes, there is little likelihood that the organization will realize its vision.

Culture Drives Performance

In an interview with the *New York Times*, Stephen Sadove, Chairman and Chief Executive of Saks, agrees that culture drives results:

"Culture drives innovation and whatever else you are trying to accomplish within a company — innovation, execution, whatever it's going to be. And that then drives results. When I talk to Wall Street, people really want to know your results, what are your strategies, what are the issues, what it is that you're doing to drive your business?

Never do you get people asking about the culture, about leadership, about the people in the organization. Yet it's the reverse, because it's the people, the leadership, and the ideas that are ultimately driving the numbers and the results.[17]

Aligning Vision and Culture

Most organizations can cite both good and bad aspects of their present culture. Things they like and things that would be better changed. From the perspective of a continuous improvement leader, the challenge and goal is to recognize and nurture those cultural aspects that contribute to achieving the vision, values, and goals of the organization and to identify and replace those aspects that do not.

Creating an Intentional Culture

Work habits, as with personal habits, are not easily changed and require more than an inspiring vision and hope for improvements. Change demands strident leadership communication and demonstration of the desired behaviors. Also required is a higher level of accountability among those holding influence across the organization.

To reorder behaviors and permanently influence the culture requires a total commitment to recognizing and rewarding desired behaviors and challenging those that are impeding progress. If

---

17   David Fechtman. "The Three Guiding Principles for Creating an Intentional Culture." *Forbes*. January, 2018.
     https://www.forbes.com/sites/forbescoachescouncil/2018/01/2
     6/the-three-guiding-principles-for-creating-an-intentional-
     culture/

there is a failure to focus on aligning the culture with the vision, improvement initiatives will flounder and the vision will never be realized.

Taking Stock

Our comparison of the differences between traditional management work practices and CI management work practices (see below) offers insight into the behavioral changes necessary to assist your initiatives.

TRADITIONAL MANAGEMENT WORK PRACTICES	CI MANAGEMENT WORK PRACTICES
Plans and instructs.	Involves and empowers.
Controls people / enforces rules.	Seeks win-win solutions / listens.
Communicates one-on-one.	Coaches and supports.
Applies top-down decision making.	Engages the whole team.
Demands respect and compliance.	Earns trust and cooperation.
Employs people's hands, not minds.	Taps people's wisdom and experience.

In the "traditional" setting, employees are told what to do and how to do it. The thinking and directing is left to the management: "it's their job." Frontline employees see themselves as singular, focused almost entirely on meeting their daily requirements. They work for an organization and don't see themselves as an integral part of it, nor contributing to its success. In the worst cases, there is an "us versus them" mentality.

In a "continuous improvement" environment, employees are viewed and treated as members of a team. Management and front line combine their knowledge and experience in pursuit of attaining the organization's vision and goals. Employees see themselves as a valued contributor to the organization's success.

Identifying What Needs to Change

Culture (how we do things around here) affects virtually each person in your organization and every aspect of the business. Conducting an honest assessment of what the culture is today and what is needed for tomorrow will clarify the work to be done. By assessing current traditions, behaviors, and work practices, you are able to generate a baseline, create actions, and measure progress, moving the organization from traditional to CI-focused.

So now that you've identified the culture changes that are needed, the question is "how do you go about doing it?" How do you successfully reorder an established culture and management practices with a different set of behaviors and rules?

Happy New Year!

Most of us are familiar with the long-standing tradition of making New Year's resolutions. Whether it is deciding to go on a diet, quit smoking, start exercising, save money, learn a new skill, or whatever it is for you, the challenge is the same. We are making a conscious effort to change our personal behavior and introduce something different into our lives. In essence, by changing our personal behaviors, we are changing our own individual culture.

When implementing a process-improvement initiative, we are pursuing a very similar goal. We intend to replace non-helpful work habits and behaviors with positive new ones *—by shifting our collective work behaviors, we are shifting our organization's culture.*

Most of us share the experience of failing to achieve a New Year's resolution — it is challenging to change behavior. Changing behaviors requires a strategic, conscious, and thoughtful effort supported by dedication and commitment. According to *U.S. News & World Report*, the failure rate for New Year resolutions is said to be about 80 percent, as most people lose their resolve by mid-February. These resolutions are our personal "flavors of the month."

Weight Watchers

Each January, the lines at the local Weight Watcher meeting stretches out the door – and for good reason – Weight Watchers gets results.

Jean Evelyn Nidetch, the founder of the Weight Watchers organization, was overweight and aspiring to lose weight. Nidetch experimented with several types of diets before achieving some success in 1961. Still facing challenges and the will power to continue, she contacted several overweight friends and founded a support group which developed into weekly classes.

This was a breakthrough for Nidetch and her friends, as they had discovered key elements to successfully changing behaviors. By creating a support group and weekly classes, they had added accountability, coaching, and engagement into what was once an individual struggle.

Nidetch's fledgling support group was incorporated on May 15, 1963 as the Weight Watchers organization. Weight Watchers has been in business for over 50 years with revenue of over $1.3 billion in 2017. Their methods are based in science and experience.[18]

---

18 weightwatchers.com. 2016 Annual Report.

Over the years, the Weight Watchers model has continued to evolve and now includes: a mobile app; daily, weekly, monthly measures; and a whole range of guidance, creative ideas, free diet advice, recipes , and even medical support where needed, to those hoping to achieve their weight-loss goals. In-depth action plans with personal coaches for skill building, strategy planning, cooking coaches, and rewards and recognition are all integral parts of the program developed to influence and shift personal behavior.

There are strong similarities in the techniques of the Weight Watchers program and the elements of "The Five Keys to Continuous Improvement." Setting goals, personal accountability, creating daily, weekly and monthly measures, training, coaching, and engaging in groups sharing ideas are the same methods used in the successful organizational change efforts with which we have been involved.

Making the connection between how the changing of personal behavior and habits relates to the changing of the collective behaviors and habits in organizations is central to creating the culture now required.

Changing Behaviors To Change Culture

Our experience is that *all successful workplace improvement programs required some shifts in culture* and the most effective way of creating that shift is through changes in work practices – in other words, people's behavior. For example, if reducing rework is the focus of a process improvement effort, and the equipment itself is not the problem, then certain changes in employee behavior need to occur. Those behavioral changes should be well thought out, engaging the people that do the work as the catalyst.

So, continuing with our example, if each incident of rework required a problem-solving session to determine what happened and why, these problem-solving sessions reflect a change in behavior – a change in the culture. If these problem-solving efforts contribute to reducing the amount of rework, then problem-solving sessions becomes the norm and a positive cultural change.

Changing behaviors can be a challenging process– here is a path we recommend:

1. **Change your own behavior first.** You are the leader of this endeavor, so all eyes will rightly be on you and others in leadership positions. Walking the talk is a critical aspect of building credibility and gaining needed support.

2. **Make a plan.** Creating a realistic plan, including the input of other key leaders, will increase the likelihood that changes in behaviors will actually occur. Your plan should include goals, measures, and an accountability process.

3. **Communicate the plan.** Share important features and explain why these changes are necessary and how they contribute to the success of the organization. Use multiple forms of communications, town halls, signage, team meetings, etc.

4. **Provide training and coaching support.** New behaviors may need to be taught and regular coaching of colleagues should be provided. Don't assume that others will know what changes are expected and remember that old habits die hard.

5. **Make changes to standards.** Make behavioral changes to Standard Operation Procedures (SOPs) and Leaders Standard Work (LSW) assignments. In doing so, you are institutionalizing new behaviors for current colleagues and those who follow.

6. **Don't make too many changes at once.** Change is not easy and if your colleagues feel overwhelmed, then more resistance is likely to occur. Be patient and supportive.

7. **Recognize and celebrate progress**. As behavior changes become apparent – celebrate! Your colleagues need to be recognized for their efforts and taking time to show appreciation is time well spent.

As a January 16, 2017 ASTD study[19] points out, accountability and incentives contribute significantly to the likelihood of successful adoption of behavioral changes. As Weight Watchers has continually proven, through daily point tracking, weekly weigh-ins, and a weight loss recognition system, it is the combination of several factors that makes the difference between success and failure.

TAKEAWAYS

▶ If an organization's culture is incompatible with its vision and strategy, then the likely result is failure!

▶ Understand the current "lay of the land" by assessing your current culture and work practices. Identify those features of each that need to shift and initiate actions to align behaviors to the vision.

▶ The best way to build a continuous improvement culture is through the changing of personal behaviors and work habits. How well these changes in behaviors and new habits are embedded will be reflected through improved performance results.

A culture assessment template is available for download at www.thefivekeys.org

19   Stacey Hanke. "Three Steps to Overcoming Resistance ." *Forbes*. August, 2018.
https://www.forbes.com/sites/forbescoachescouncil/2018/08/14/three-steps-to-overcoming-resistance/#7b97ec485eae

SECTION 2
THE FIVE KEYS

THE FIVE KEYS

The real challenge for CI Leaders is not introducing a cycle of successful one-off improvement initiatives, but rather to imbed a dynamic culture, one that inspires colleagues to find ways of improving on a daily basis. This is the heavy lifting! To accomplish this, almost without exception, demands a change in culture — and culture change rarely comes quickly nor easily; it takes time and perseverance. This work is not showy and glitzy. It is the daily commitment to fostering an organization where improvement and innovation are valued and sustained. This is the crucial work of the CI Leader and The Five Keys are here to assist you in making it happen.

This book was inspired by our puzzlement as to why two seemingly "identical" sister manufacturing sites producing the same products, at the same time, with the same equipment, with the same suppliers and customers, with the same internal support, engaging a very similar workforce, working with the same CI consultants introducing the same methodologies, lean tools and practices and reporting to the same organizational hierarchy would experience vastly different results.

As longstanding advocates for continuous improvement, we were always acutely aware of the critical role culture plays in determining organizational success. What surprised us, after analyzing each variable at the two "identical" manufacturing sister sites, was our conclusion: that **culture was the only significant difference between these two sites.**

And most importantly, differences in culture resided in five distinct categories:

▶ Leadership

▶ Engagement

▶ Goal Alignment

▶ Accountability

▶ Resources

Thus, **"The 5 Keys."**

These "keys" have proven to us to be the most impactful elements in founding a culture of continuous improvement. All five are equally important; they overlap and work together in concert and all five are necessary in the creation of a vibrant and enduring improvement-focused culture. This is not to say that solely embracing The Five Keys will guarantee success. However, what we have learned and believe deeply is that without these "keys," the likelihood of that success is improbable.

In this section, you will learn more about these Five Keys and how to introduce, nurture and sustain them. We also describe and suggest effective means for deploying each of The Five Keys in your organization. Having a well-considered and comprehensive approach to *instill all Five Keys is essential.*

🔍 CASE STUDY: THE TWO SISTER SITES

We initially introduced a high engagement team-based work system at two alike manufacturing sites. The process aligned goals and measures throughout each site, established team roles, norms, and reporting structure throughout and provided a structured process and tools for continuous improvement, accountability, and problem-solving. After launching the program, we visited the sites each quarter, spending two days auditing progress, training various lean tools, coaching the leadership and frontlines while providing detailed recommendations for improvement. Each year, after the one-week launch, eight days were spent on site – two days each quarter.

These two sites were not alone in this corporate mandated endeavor. Dozens of other business sites, located around the globe, were also required to develop a continuous improvement culture with a goal of being fully implemented in five to seven years. It was also recognized that each individual site would be entering at differing levels of maturity and understanding relative to improvement tools and a continuous improvement culture. So, the quarterly visits would prove vital in providing the time necessary to initiate new concepts, tools and behaviors.

At the five – seven year mark, all sites had the option to individually continue their relationship with our consulting group or to rely on the internal capacity that was developed over time. Some sites continued our quarterly arrangement, some met at irregular intervals and others moved forward on their own. Sites 1 and 2 continued quarterly visits for very different reasons.

Site 1 had determined that quarterly visits added value to the site. These two-day visits had become a part of the "this is the way we do business" routine. These visits allowed for a reassessment of progress and projects, to focus on more complex problems and to grow internal capacity.

Site 2 was making progress, and relied on quarterly visits to keep inching CI culture forward, reinforce new behaviors, provide coaching, mentor project leaders, teach tools and guide next steps.

Over the ten-year period that we worked with these two sites, Site 1 became the company's model for continuous improvement and sustainability, while Site 2 continued struggling with a litany of performance, safety, and personnel issues.

This dilemma crystalized for us the necessity to determine, for ourselves, the differences between these two sites and chart a path of course-correction. If we could solve this puzzle, the solutions could provide value to all our clients and be shared with others in the continuous improvement community. At the end of each chapter of The Five Keys (Leadership, Engagement, Goal Alignment, Accountability and Resources), under the heading *Two Sister Sites - Case Study - Solving the Puzzle*, David provides first-person examples of differences noted between the two sister sites as it pertains to that particular key.

LEADERSHIP

SET DIRECTION	COMMUNICATE	GENERATE COMMITMENT	BUILD CAPACITY

Culture is not the most important thing -- It's the only thing"

—Costco Co-Founder and retired CEO Jim Sinegal

"Leadership is a function in the organization, rather than the trait of an individual. It is distributed among the members of a group or organization, and is not automatically vested in the chairman or the person with the formal authority. Good leadership and good membership therefore blend into each other in an effective organization."

—Edgar Schein[20]

There has never been more attention paid to leadership and leading than today. There are over 50,000 books on Amazon with "leadership" in the title. Global corporate training spending has been steadily increasing over the past several years, with a total spend of $366.2 billion in 2018. The leadership training market is one of the only Leadership & Development markets that has experienced growth independent of economic trends year after year. Training Industry research estimates that in 2018, organizations around the world spent about $3.4 billion

---

20   Edgar Schein. *Organizational Culture and Leadership.* (San Francisco: Josey-Bass, 1985).

with leadership development solutions and program vendors.[21] This tremendous interest in effective leadership is not surprising, because leading is central to the overall performance and financial success of organizations.

Technology and competition have reshaped the business landscape.[22] Established business icons like Pan Am, Toshiba, Radio Shack, Blockbuster, Borders, Toys "R" Us, Bethlehem Steel, Eastern Airlines, Woolworths, E.F. Hutton, Standard Oil, and General Foods, to name just a few, have virtually disappeared. And, the record is even worse for startup companies. Based on a 2017 study of the Harvard Business School, the failure rate for startups after five years was over fifty percent and seventy percent after ten years. In a study by Statistic Brain, the failure rate of all U.S. companies after five years was over 50 percent, and over 70 percent after 10 years.[23]

These sobering facts demonstrate that there is no guarantee for business longevity. As good as the product, service, and staff may be, circumstances change and an organization's ability to shift to get in front of those challenges is paramount. With this awareness, *insightful business leaders recognize that continuous improvement, in every aspect of their enterprise, is essential to their long-term competitiveness and viability.*

21   The Leadership Training Market. March, 2019.
     https://trainingindustry.com/wiki/leadership/the-leadership-training-market/

22   Jeff Moore. "101 on Digital Tranformation: What is it & How is it Reshaping Business?" August, 2019.
     https://www.bairesdev.com/blog/digital-transformation-reshaping-businesses

23   Statistic Brain Research Institute. Startup Business Failure By Industry, May 2017. https://www.statisticbrain.com/startup-failure-by-industry/

Leading Change Efforts

The need to continually improve is unrelenting and should be at the forefront of every organization's agenda across the globe. Most companies are somewhere on a path either launching such initiatives, currently immersing themselves in ongoing efforts, or having stalled or mothballed their attempts, waiting perhaps for a more opportune time.

But regardless of where your organization is on the CI spectrum, the mandate to continually improve is not going away. For many businesses and organizations, long-term success depends on how well and how quickly they are able to adapt and keep pace with their competitors. This requirement will only intensify in coming years, testing the commitment and ingenuity of business leaders and their colleagues.

Better Tools – Better Outcomes

As challenging as the future appears, leaders of continuous improvement have plenty to cheer about! Today, proven tools, methods, and techniques for initiating improvements are readily available for practically every business and industry. Continuous improvement approaches run the gamut and without question, generate improvements.[24]

But, at the end of the day, it is not the tools, methods, or the tens-of-thousands of smart dedicated CI professionals that ultimately determine the long-term success and sustainability of CI initiatives. *Having spent decades in the trenches, educated in the methodologies and having researched the reasons why some change efforts blossom while others wither and die, the following insights hold true.*

---

24   KaiNexus. 2020. https://www.kainexus.com/roi-of-continuous-improvement

▶ Absent the adoption of an organizational culture that embraces change and is committed to continual improvement, the program will eventually die. Almost without exception, this mindset to constantly improve is required for sustained success.

▶ Steadfast leadership is required to establish and maintain this culture.

In this chapter, we will explore:

▶ Leadership Models

▶ The Work of Leadership

▶ Leadership Behaviors, Standard Work, and SOPs

▶ Building Internal Capacity

▶ Individual and Team Goals

▶ Resistance

▶ Leadership versus Management

▶ Expanding Your Leadership Footprint

Leadership Models

Over the last century leaders and their organizations have been exposed to scores of differing leadership models including:

Scientific Management	Great Man and Trust
Lewin Leadership Styles	Charismatic
Contingency	Participative
Leader-Member Exchange	Situational
Path-Goal	Servant
Transformational	Authentic
Transactional	Full Range

and dozens of lesser-known theories.

Plenty of good advice has been offered over the decades by great theorists and behavioral science practitioners. Attempting to digest it all will leave you with plenty of good advice and possibly a headache. In fact, differing models, fads, and trends in leadership are often cyclical. A newer model emerges to replace the existing one.

Today, Transformational Leadership (*a theory of leadership where a leader works with teams to identify needed change, creating a vision to guide the change through inspiration, and executing the change in tandem with committed members of a group*) currently enjoys high marks in "how to lead." But as soon as the shine is off, there will be another hot model to replace it.

While we applaud the Transformation Leadership model as well as others, there is no "one size fits all" approach for leaders. So, it is not our purpose to coax leaders to adopt a particular model of leading. Instead, we focus on the critical work of leaders, regardless of their individual style, one that provides an organization with clarity, inspiration, and a roadmap that delivers a significant advantage over their competitors.

The Critical Work of Leadership in Continuous Improvement Efforts

> *"Leadership is the capacity to translate vision into reality"*
>
> **— Warren Bennis**

The work of leadership, as applied in continuous improvement efforts, boils down to four primary activities:

▶ Setting Direction

▶ Communicating

▶ Generating Commitment

▶ Unleashing Internal Capacity

Setting Direction - Leading the Way

Setting direction, whether for an entire organizational transformation or simply the introduction of a garden-variety continuous improvement initiative, the preparation for creating a vision and strategy is much the same.

In order to set the direction and create a realistic plan, it is imperative to gain a thorough understanding of certain base elements, which are:

▶ The current and future requirements of key stakeholders (i.e., customers, management, employees, suppliers, competitors, unions, community, others).

▶ What your competitors are doing to meet their stakeholders' requirements.

▶ Industry innovations and trends.

▶ An honest assessment of how your organization is presently positioned.

▶ Other likely challenges.

An accurate assessment is vital as many future decisions and plans will emanate from these findings. Establishing a competent task force can help ensure a comprehensive assessment is developed.

Upon completion of this assessment, often compiled by a task group, you and your team can now begin to develop an inspiring vision and strategy plan with specific objectives, benchmarks, and goals necessary for success. By conscientiously working through the various steps in a comprehensive planning process, you are gaining the knowledge and clarity required to inform and persuade your colleagues that the new path being charted is one that is important to them and vital for the organization.

Even small change efforts deserve the same forethought and insight necessary to optimize success.

Create a Vision

A well-articulated vision can act as a "North Star" for an organization. It provides clear direction, inspires confidence in the future, and establishes the basis for developing a comprehensive strategy. Unlike strategies and goals, a vision remains constant and seldom changes. Furthermore, the likelihood of an endeavor becoming the "flavor of the month" is diminished as the vision answers many questions before they are asked and communicates to the organization that necessary resources will be provided.

Developing Vision and Strategy

There is not a "one right way" approach to fashioning a vision and strategy, but important aspects include the need to be:

▶ Future-based and Inspiring: Describes a desirable picture of a future state that energizes and engages those involved.

▶ Appealing: Speaks to both internal and external stakeholders.

▶ Challenging yet Realistic: The vision should be a stretch, but can be accomplished - not pie in the sky.

▶ Clear and Precise: Keep it simple, but provide enough detail so others know where this is headed.

▶ Specific: Provides clear and understandable goals, measures, and timelines.

▶ Answers the "WHY": Communicates the reason this change is important.

Communicating - Developing an Effective Program

Effectively communicating your change initiative and adequately anticipating and addressing colleagues' questions establishes the grounds for a successful program.

We have repeatedly found that the development and implementation of a comprehensive communication strategy is often given little attention or is disregarded entirely. We have learned that upfront, honest, and practical communication weighs heavily on how the change initiative is viewed and significantly impacts the speed of adoption.

When communication is lacking or poorly executed, a void is created and is open to misconceptions, rumors and even sabotage.

Figure 1: Departments meet to identify strategies, objectives and goals.

The Leap of Faith

Employees, from the executive level to the front lines, understandably are cautious about lending their endorsement and support to something new and unexplored. A rational survival instinct of "how does this affect me?" comes into play, often unconsciously, in all of us.

So, what does it take for a typical member of your organization to take that leap of faith and willingly commit and genuinely support a new vision? We have found that tailoring your communications to address legitimate questions and colleagues apprehensions up front, before you launch, will help mitigate fear and resistance.

Listed below are the several aspects of communicating the vision and plan that will assist you in addressing the natural fears, spoken and unspoken, held by many of your colleagues. These factors can impact significantly the adoption or rejection of change efforts. These include:

▶ Make Clear the Vision: A vision describes a future state and must be shared with and adopted by your colleagues. It is vital that each person understands the vision and is able to share it with others in a way that will matter to them. People don't need every detail, but they want to know what the vision means and how this change affects them and their work. It is important to remember that your colleagues are seeking information from a person they know and trust. Be well prepared to share the information in three minutes or less. (see "elevator speech" in the goal alignment chapter)

▶ The Why: People within your organization must fully comprehend "why" the need for change exists, and the "why" must be compelling to them and important for the organization. Explain and demonstrate the reasons that the status quo is no longer satisfactory. Share data that proves the necessity for change. Inform them of rising expectations from your stakeholders, especially customers. Share industry data and what your competition is doing. Remember, if I don't know "why" change is important, then the "how" really doesn't matter!

▶ Continuously Communicate: We have yet to find an organization that communicates too much. Using all communication forms, channels, and techniques available exponentially increases support and participation. Update progress regularly, and share successes, failures, and challenges. Acknowledging disappointments and adversity demonstrates honesty and confirms real-life issues that need to be overcome.

▶ Make the vision a focal point demonstrating pride and commitment. Use every means at your disposal. Consider signage, newsletters, bulletin boards, intranet, one-on-ones, town hall meetings, etc. Some organizations have found giveaways like t-shirts, coffee mugs, etc., add to the excitement.

▶ Spell Out the Benefits: People must clearly see how this "change" will improve their organization and how it benefits them personally. Share early wins, goals reached, and milestones met. Connect these positive results to personal and organizational benefits. Recognize good performance.

▶ Keep It Simple: Your message should be straightforward and uncomplicated. Too much detail is confusing and unsettling. Share the basics: What, How, Who and When.

▶ Be Patient: Don't expect people to readily adopt a new innovation or change initiative. Your organization's culture and behaviors have hardened over time – sometimes decades. Changes to these habits and customs take time and effort. With commitment, reinforcement, and through example, colleagues will join in the effort - over time. (See the Diffusion of Innovations in the Roots Section.)

▶ Seek Feedback: You may be employing all the best methods of communicating the various aspects of your change effort throughout your organization, but there is more. In order to keep your fingers on the pulse, create opportunities for colleagues to provide you with their feedback – welcoming both good and bad. Learn from your colleagues what they think, their worries, and desires. Share what you learn with other leaders and resolve legitimate concerns.

Because you are immersed in the day-to-day details of the effort, you are likely to be quite sensitive to any criticism or advice you may receive from your colleagues. However, creating an environment of trust, where differences of opinion and criticism are welcomed, allows others to feel that they are being heard and they can openly speak their minds.

At the end of the day, listening and acting on colleague's feedback generates greater ownership and support. Good communication is a two-way street – you need feedback, both positive and negative.

Generating Commitment, Wholehearted, Without Reservation

"Until one is committed, there is hesitancy, the chance to draw back, always ineffectiveness. Concerning all acts of initiative and creation, there is one elementary truth the ignorance of which kills countless ideas and splendid plans: that the moment one definitely commits oneself, then providence moves too. All sorts of things occur to help one that would never otherwise have occurred. A whole stream of events issues from the decision, raising in one's favor all manner of unforeseen incidents, meetings and material assistance which no man could have dreamed would have come his way. I have learned a deep respect for one of Goethe's couplets: Whatever you can do, or dream you can, begin it! Boldness has genius, magic, and power in it."

— W.H. Murray, on the Scottish Himalayan Expedition on the 1951 Everest Reconnaissance[25]

---

25   W.H. Murray. *The Evidence of Things Not Seen: A Mountaineer's Tale.* (London: Baton Wicks . 2002).

Walking the Talk

Nothing can undermine commitment to a new endeavor more than leaders who say one thing and then do another. The leaders' behavior speaks more loudly to employees and customers than any words on the wall could ever say.

Looking back on one of the most outrageous examples of leaders' actions not aligning with their strategy comes immediately to mind as we recall the crises experienced in 2008 in the US auto industry:

All Big Three automakers, General Motors, Ford and Chrysler, were in desperate straits with the prospect of bankruptcy only months away at Chrysler and General Motors. The CEOs appealed to the U.S. Congress to appear before them. Their goal was to explain their plight and secure a $25 billion taxpayer bailout.

On November 18, 2008, all three CEOs traveled to Washington, D.C., to explain their company's financial dilemma and ask for help. The CEOs chose to fly in their corporate jets from Detroit to the Capital. Rick Wagoner flew in GM's $36 million luxury aircraft to tell members of Congress that the company is burning through cash, asking for $10-12 billion for GM alone.

Some Members of Congress were alerted to their air travel by the press, and were outraged:

"There is a delicious irony in seeing private luxury jets flying into Washington, D.C., and people coming off of them with tin cups in their hand, saying that they're going to be trimming down and streamlining their businesses," Rep. Gary Ackerman, D-New York, told the chief executive officers of Ford, Chrysler and General Motors at a hearing of the House Financial Services Committee. "It's almost like seeing a guy show up at the soup kitchen in high hat and tuxedo. It kind of makes you a little bit suspicious."

He added, "couldn't you all have downgraded to first class or jet-pooled or something to get here? It would have at least sent a message that you do get it." [26]

The cost of the corporate jet ride for Mr. Wagoner was $20,000 versus a ride in Coach at $288 and First Class at $837. [27]

The CEOs left that day chastised and without a vote on the bailout being taken. For a follow-up hearing, again appealing to the Senate Finance Committee, all three CEOs drove to Washington in hybrid vehicles!

Back Home Example

While the auto leader story is extreme, a memorable example of talk not matching the walk occurred at a steel manufacturing site where we recently worked. Here, a 5S Visual Workplace initiative was begun and led by the Quality Manager. The aim of this 5S program was "to create a safe, pleasant, organized and efficient workplace by eliminating waste and making work easier."

Picture this: the office of the quality manager was in a main hallway traveled by all employees – the door always open. The office was a pig sty. Samples of materials were piled from the floor to the window ledge. Grease and oil dripped from the samples and covered the floor. Manuals and paperwork were piled high on the desk and cabinet drawers were overflowing and could not be closed. It was clear that this office had not been cleaned and organized in years. The joke in the plant was that this manager was the lead on the new 5S Visual Workplace program. Sadly, it

---

26 Josh Lewis. November, 2008.
    https://www.cnn.com/2008/US/11/19/autos.ceo.jets/
27 Brian Ross & Joseph Rhee. November, 2008.
    https://abcnews.go.com/Blotter/WallStreet/story?id=6285739&
    page=1

begged the question, are the employees here really expected to take this effort seriously?

Behavior Leads the Way

"The most powerful leadership tool you have is your own personal example."

— John Wooden,
(American Basketball Player – Former Head Coach of UCLA Team

Every change initiative requires certain changes in behaviors. But changing, "how we do things around here" isn't easy and requires persistence, discipline, and leading by example. The importance of leadership, demonstrating and adopting different behaviors that support the new vision, is required and the impact cannot be overstated. For example, if frontline daily team meetings are required, the leader in that area could attend and participate each week. Where employees are responsible for keeping their area neat and orderly, the leader could visibly maintain their own workspace and take part in area housekeeping audits. If innovation and improvement ideas are encouraged, the leader could take an active role in ensuring that improvement recommendations are promptly assessed and those endorsed are implemented.

Standard Work

A proven and effective way to instill a behavior change is through the adoption of "standard work," which we define as a list of tasks that must be done to support the desired changes. By establishing standardized tasks, employees across the organization observe and participate in actionizing new behaviors consistent with the vision. For example, if the vision was one that initiated a 5S - Visual Workplace Process, some typical standard tasks might include:

Tasks	Who	Frequency
Conduct 5S Audit	Supervisor	2 / week
5S Training Talk	Supervisor/Team Leader	Weekly
Machine Inspection	Supervisor / Machine Operator	1 per week
Red Tag Event / Signposting	Team Members	Quarterly
Update Opportunity Board	Team Leader/Members	Weekly
Checklist Evaluation	Area Manager	Monthly
5 minute "end of day" shine up	Team Members	Daily

By clearly defining "standard work" for the 5S Process, new behaviors are being introduced that are necessary to support the vision. The commitment now becomes clear.

Standard Operating Procedures - SOP

Standard Operating Procedures is a term and a practice many of us are familiar with. SOPs are simply a document that defines how to perform a task. By following a set procedure, safety and performance compliance is assured. Modifying SOPs to support a vision encourages changes in behavior necessary to accomplish the new goals.

A typical SOP details a number of compliance topics, but an example of adding to a manufacturing SOP to support a 5S Visual Workplace process might include:

▶ Ensure only materials for today's work remain in your work area.

▶ Your tools and instruments are sorted, labelled, and on your workbench.

▶ All scrap and defective goods are immediately placed in the "scrap bin."

▶ Your workbench and the floor in your work area is free of dirt, oil, and water.

▶ The "dead man" switch is labelled and tested at the start of each shift.

▶ Work in Progress or WIP is clearly identified and neatly stored.

▶ 5 minutes from the end of shift – "shine up" time.

In this example, by modifying the SOP to support the 5S Process, you are impacting, in a positive way, people's behaviors and thereby gently shifting your organization's culture. What leadership behaviors do you believe must become the new standard in order to shift your organization's culture?

Building Internal Capacity - Unleashing the Talent Within

Today's business environment requires organizations to utilize the experience and talents of their employees as never before, and the resulting positive bottom-line impact is undeniable. (see chapter on Employee Engagement)

Creating a workplace culture where employees are willing or even eager to assume greater responsibility and control is a challenge each Continuous Improvement leader faces. In most traditional organizations, solving problems and initiating improvements was the sole province of the management group.

With this historical backdrop, expanding the role of the rank and file to participate in problem solving and initiating improvements is sometimes viewed with suspicion. The front lines may interpret these changes as increasing their workload, while some members of management may see the changes as an infringement and it's "their job" and consider it a threat.

Our experience has repeatedly shown that, given the opportunity, colleagues of all stripes rise to the challenges and continually surprise with their talents.

We suggest these few positive steps, regardless of how progressive or traditional your current organizational environment, in order to earn the confidence of both management and the frontline:

Build Trust

People will not follow those they do not trust. As the visible leader in your change effort, your colleagues must learn to trust you. By doing what you say and saying what you do repeatedly, time after time, you stay true to your word. Following through when you say you will demonstrates your commitment and invites others to do likewise.

Disappointments in the past, promises made and broken, flavors of the month, etc., are on the minds of many when launching a new change effort. Acknowledging past failures (all organizations have had them) contributes to your leadership's credibility and provides guideposts for this new effort. Learning from mistakes and making course corrections are the hallmarks of great leaders and great organizations.

Always Speak the Truth

Give your colleagues the straight facts — sharing what you know about the status of the initiative, its successes as well as struggles. Updates are not always going to be good news. While it is not pleasant to share setbacks and mistakes, your colleagues deserve to know the details and are quite capable of dealing with it. Chances are they already have heard the bad news as that type of data typically travels much faster than the good.

By telling it as it is, you gain respect and support. When you speak the truth to colleagues, they in turn will share what is really going on — things you might never uncover. Your credibility is paramount, so protect it. If there are things you cannot discuss or share with others, simply say so and reveal what you can. Your colleagues will appreciate your candor and straightforward approach.

Foster Ownership

As a leader in the effort, you are heavily invested in its success. But real sustainability lies in creating genuine ownership among the majority of your colleagues at every level. When your co-workers assume ownership of their daily work and their results, they typically exhibit greater responsibility, make well-informed decisions, improve their performance, and work to solve problems. Ownership is further enhanced when good performance is recognized and celebrated.

Establish Individual and Team Goals That Support the Vision

Every vision should be accompanied by a strategy, goals, and milestones. Creating a clear line of sight between the strategic objectives laid out in the vision to the daily goals, measures, and work of employees highlights the importance of the change and adds individual accountability to the system. The accomplishment of these individual or team goals connects to the vision, and should be readily acknowledged and rewarded.

Visually displaying positive results and milestones reached demonstrates ongoing organizational commitment and support. Demand accountability and recognize good performance. Share successes and give credit where it is due. Celebrate gains regularly.

Dealing with Resistance - Normal and Predictable

When a change initiative is introduced, most people are somewhere on a scale ranging from reluctant to resistant. Your colleagues may eventually support the vision or they may not. Because a new vision requires change, and change can be uncomfortable, each individual will assess the effort based on their individual criteria. Like it or not, *every change effort is weighed, positively or negatively, by each individual in the organization.*

Status Quo Bias

"Status quo bias refers to the phenomenon of preferring that one's environment and/or situation remains as it already is." The term was first introduced in 1988 by Samuelson and Zeckhauser, who demonstrated status quo bias through a series of decision-making experiments. Their research identified several different possible reasons for status quo bias of which "loss aversion" in the work environment appears most applicable.[28]

Loss Aversion

"When individuals make decisions, they *weigh the potential for loss more heavily than the potential for gain.* Thus, when looking at a set of choices, they focus more on what they could lose by abandoning the status quo than on what they could gain by trying something new." [29]

28 William Samuelson and Richard Zeckhauser. "Status Quo Bias in Decision Making." *Journal of Risk and Uncertainty*. 1988. vol. 1, no. 1, pp. 7-59.

29 Cynthia Vinney. Status Quo Bias: What it Means and How it Affect Your Behavior. December, 2019. thoughtco.com/status-quo-bias-4172981

Resistance to change is universal and applies equally to top leadership, managers, supervisors, and front-line colleagues. As humans, we prefer sameness and predictability to uncertainty and chance. This holds true even knowing that the only sure thing in life is change itself - yet we, in our deepest fibers, find it unsettling and stressful.

Factors of Resistance

There is an assortment of other reasons why people resist change aside from the deep-seated desire for maintaining the status quo. As your colleagues weigh the risk and reward aspects of the proposed initiative, they also recall their past experiences with change efforts and how that played out over the long run. Were they a winner or loser at the end of the day? Did the changes make their jobs easier or harder? Did the effort fulfill the improvement claims? Did colleagues have adequate time to take on required tasks? Was their change leader trustworthy and honest with them? All of these and many other concerns are real for you and your colleagues and set the backdrop for this new initiative.

As legitimate and impactful as these experiences and lessons may be, we have found that the leading reason why people resist change comes down to: FEAR! Not that anyone would admit it, nor would it be labeled as "fear," but any new improvement initiative, whether major or minor, often leads to changes in method, manpower, technology, process, and/or product. Couple these changes with past experiences in previous efforts, hoped-for improvements in efficiency and cost reduction, and this "new program" may spell "loss" to many. While the "fears" for each individual varies, fear often falls into three main areas:

▶ Fear of Job Loss: Will this change undermine my current position? Will I have my job after this new initiative is implemented? What if I try and fail?

▶ Fear of the Unknown: What changes will I need to make? How will my workload and responsibilities change? What will my supervisor demand from me? Will they help me? Will I be embarrassed?

▶ Fear for my Future? Am I capable of learning new skills that may be required? Will they train me? Will this provide opportunities for me? What's in it for me?

From your colleague's perspective, both management and front-line, a change initiative upends the status quo and adds elements of unpredictability. Most individuals subscribe to the old adage: "The devil you know is better than the devil you don't." This is simply human nature. While these three "fear factors" are not the only sources of resistance, they are central for most people.

Figure 2: Group Leader lessens resistance by explaining graphs to her colleagues.

Combating the Forces of Fear and Resistance

Change is unsettling both to individuals and departments. Fears and concerns of all types haunt many, as colleagues are asked to adopt and implement new behaviors and/or different work practices. While these concerns may not surface in a public forum, team meetings or even in the break room, it doesn't mean they don't exist. Worries are personal and, if left unaddressed, often delay or even sabotage much-needed change.

In addition to including a comprehensive approach to dealing with resistance in your planning, you and other leaders can make a huge difference in the adoption of your CI initiative by:

▶ Making yourself available: Go out of your way to speak to people you suspect are struggling. Their behavior and lack of engagement is a clue that something is amiss.

▶ Speaking privately and confidentially: Encourage colleagues to share their discomfort.

▶ Adopt a genuine sense of curiosity: Listen to learn how they view the new program. Let them know you care and their concerns matter.

▶ Not arguing or attempting to persuade: Look instead for clues as to what it would take to bring them on board.

▶ Share examples of similar successful change efforts where fears existed but were never realized.

▶ Provide whatever help you have available: Training, on-the-job coaching, classes, etc.

▶ Being patient and supportive: Recognize that your colleagues want to contribute and need to be assured that they have what it takes.

Keep in mind that if one person is resistant to the change for a specific reason, you can rest assured that there are others who feel that same way. Making a personal effort to assuage their concerns will help legitimize their worries and mitigate unneeded resistance.

Always recognize that a "new" initiative brings with it, a legitimate sense of concern. Whether executive or front-line, your colleagues will wonder if they have the ability, time and competence to perform new tasks demanded of them. **It takes courage to jump aboard.** Assure them if you can. If training and/or other support will be provided, they need to know. **Use each opportunity to not only talk about what the change requires but also discuss what will remain the same and not change.**

Hearing from a trusted colleague is reassuring and appreciated. Additionally, CI leaders should attempt to identify other potential areas of resistance and address those if possible. Don't dismiss these resistance factors as insignificant. These factors are very real and threatening to some of your colleagues. Address them up front. It is better to take them head on then to fight this battle later.

"If you are a leader, your team watches you. Do you actually mean what you say? The team will continuously look for clues and inconsistencies in your message and your actions. If they find those inconsistencies, you'll soon witness a rise in fear. It doesn't take much fear to wipe out that feel-safe culture, and suddenly you're commanding a being-safe culture."

—Richard Sheridan, author and CEO at Menlo Innovations, which has won the Alfred P. Sloan Award for Business Excellence in Workplace

Consistency Leads to Sustainment

Inconsistency in our organization may be the quickest method of quashing a CI initiative. A clear message, supported with consistent actions, defines the expectations and standards that drive continuous improvement programs. Employees need to know what to expect and what is asked of them. Mixed messages and grey areas inspire the variability within organizations that can undermine the desired results. Defined standards, supported by accountability, stabilize that daily rhythm of continuous improvement.

While there will always be occasions of upset and disruption in every organization, a CI culture provides the process to address these disruptions and abnormalities. That process and new routines, can become that one dependable and constant factor in a world of chaos that any level of leadership or employee can lean on in a moment of crisis.

Utilizing tools such as coaching, visual management and reward and recognition provide an organization the opportunity to alleviate fear, encourage ownership, shift cultural habits and foster engagement. These tools are part of that daily CI rhythm and consistency necessary to foster a safe environment, close the gaps and sustain a CI culture.

Leadership Versus Management (The Work)

Recognizing the differences between leading and managing provides us with additional clarity on the roles and responsibilities that each play in organizations. In the grid below those differences become distinct.

The Differing Roles of Leadership and Management

	LEADERSHIP Leading	MANAGEMENT Implementing
Setting Direction	<ul><li>Assess key stakeholder's current and future needs.</li><li>Incorporate industry trends.</li><li>Anticipate competitors.</li><li>Create a vision for the future.</li><li>Develop strategies and goals.</li><li>Provide resources.</li></ul>	<ul><li>Managers add detail to the strategy.</li><li>Align systems and manage efficiencies.</li><li>Develop budgets/manpower.</li><li>Establish policies and processes.</li><li>Ensure predictability.</li></ul>

THE FIVE KEYS

	LEADERSHIP Leading	MANAGEMENT Implementing
Communica- ting Effectively	• Communicate the vision throughout using all methods of communication – make clear why this is vital. • Assure colleagues that the leadership is in this with them. • Share what support and help will be provided. • Explain what is hoped to be accomplished.	• Explain the changes required and what will remain the same. • Allow time for one-on-ones and team meetings. • Answer questions. • Seek feedback to share with other managers.
Generating Commitment	• Lead by example. • Recognize and promote supporters of the change effort. • Address managers and supervisors who are barriers to the effort. • Require accountability. • Reward successes.	• Address colleague's fears. • Solve problems. • Connect tasks and goals to the vision /and strategies. • Instill accountability.
Building Internal Capacity "Unleashing the Talent Within"	• Align systems to support effort. • Delegate authority. • Spend time on the frontlines. • Remove obstacles to engagement.	• Train, coach and oversee. • Recognize good performance. • Delegate authority. • Implement good ideas.

'Not My Job to Lead'

Keep in mind that it is easy, safe and convenient for some members in an organization to step back and defer responsibility for leading change to the executive level. "That's why they pay them the big bucks" is often heard. Unfortunately, change is not that convenient nor simple. To be a success, the commitment of individuals at every level of the organization is vital. It is not just the executives who will suffer if your initiative fails - the entire organization suffers and the impact of the failure becomes shared from the board room to the break room.

Expanding Your 'Leadership' Footprint

Historically, the responsibility for implementing change initiatives has fallen squarely on the shoulders of the executive leadership group. The long-held notion that authority, rank and title would automatically equip an organization's leaders with the knowledge, ability, and tools to drive continuous improvement is incomplete. By placing the success or failure solely on their heads, we handicap our organization's change initiatives from the very outset.

We know from experience, that no matter how competent and far-sighted a group of executive leaders and their managers may be, their sphere of influence and ability to drive improvements is limited. Herein, lies an opportunity.

If your situation is like most, within your organization there are men and women in the ranks who are early adopters of change and natural leaders among their peers. These rank-and-filers have the ability and willingness to influence and motivate their colleagues in working toward achieving common goals. It is critical for the success of your initiative to identify these people. Here's how:

Combining Technical and People Skills

When looking for colleagues to bolster your leadership team, we typically look for rank and filers holding both technical subject matter knowledge combined with certain people skills.

Technical qualifications are related to practical experience; knowledge and abilities related specifically to the improvement effort. For instance, if the improvement focus is "improving the billing process," then someone who is familiar with the many differing aspects of the invoicing and customer awareness should be considered a candidate to help with the change initiative.

As important as these technical skills are, the ideal candidate should also be able to relate and interact well and lead their billing area colleagues.

The three people skills that we find most important in expanding the leadership footprint are:

Integrity:

▶ Keeps their word

▶ Shows respect for others

▶ Accountable

▶ Trustworthy

Collaborative:

▶ Shares data and information with teammates

▶ Colleagues have an equal voice / Consensus decisions are preferred

▶ Doesn't need to be the center of attention

▶ Interacts well with other departments

Problem Solver:

▶ Focused - zeros in on the root cause

▶ Open-minded and curious / deals well with complex challenges

▶ Looks for opportunities

▶ Follows through with implementation

These individuals can assist your effort in ways that leadership simply cannot. They carry the perspectives of other front-line colleagues and bring different voices to the conversation. Consider how you might engage them in your efforts, being careful not to undercut or offend those charged with some similar duties. Having a cadre of "go-to" people can accelerate and energize the implementation effort. Find Them.

LEADERSHIP TAKEAWAYS

▶ Culture Trumps Everything

▶ Lacking the adoption of an organizational culture that embraces change and is committed to continual improvement, the program will die. Almost without exception, a major change in culture is required for sustained success.

▶ Steadfast leadership is required to establish and maintain this culture.

▶ The Work of Leaders is:

- Setting Direction

- Communicating

- Generating Commitment

- Building Internal Capacity

▶ Expand Your Leadership Footprint: natural leaders (people with influence) are in your midst –LOOK FOR THEM

The Leadership Behaviors template is available for download at www.thefivekeys.org

CASE STUDY: THE TWO SISTER SITES
SOLVING THE PUZZLE

Leadership: the ability to influence and motivate a group of people to work toward achieving a common goal.

Competent leadership skills are rooted in the proper balance of leading and engaging other members while managing the execution of projects, tasks, and duties. Leadership at Site 1 understood their role.

In the early days of their CI implementation, you would not have guessed that Site 1 would become the model of CI culture within their company. In North America, there were nearly a dozen sites with different business functions and sectors. And worldwide, there were dozens more.

For the first several years, Site 1 progress remained middle of the pack, undistinguished from other global business sites. In fact, some company locations were recognized for their quick and effective integration of CI, based upon company performance measures and corresponding audits. What ultimately set Site 1 apart, was their Leader's focus on being a model for employees. Though this approach did not produce quick results, it penetrated deep into the long-term psyche of the site.

Like most busy manufacturing sites, it can be difficult securing the time necessary to gather an entire leadership team together for CI sessions. However, this was never an issue at Site 1. In the early stages of the program, the entire leadership team would attend every session with each frontline group that I conducted. This level of commitment worked on many levels; the Leadership team understood the program and tools, it displayed that Leadership supported the program, and most importantly, the Leadership

Team was the first group to embrace the change in behaviors requested at the site.

As the years went on, building internal capacity with more advanced improvement tools became a focus. The same dedication continually displayed by the Leadership Team was now evident among all team members. Time constraints never became an issue.

The ever-growing importance of continuous improvement among the leadership team at Site 1 is reflected in the following short story: When beginning the CI journey, I assisted the Leadership Team in the development of their specific mission statement. What they decided upon, was a mission very similar to that of other Company business sites across the globe: to produce their products safely, on-time, and cost effectively for their customers.

After seven years with the same mission, the Team requested that I facilitate a session to develop a new mission statement. It seemed that the old mission no longer fit the team. The mission statement they crafted that day reflected a deep understanding of CI Culture and captured their spirit. The new mission no longer focused solely on the products produced, but instead zeroed in on their role as leaders: *fostering a culture of growth, continuous learning, safety, problem solving and coaching.* They knew if they were to stay true to their mission, the results would take care of themselves.

Despite our advice, to the contrary, Site 2 Leadership took a very "hands off" approach to their continuous improvement initiatives. Leadership there cited, time and time again, that one of the principles of CI is the engagement of the front-line team members. This proclamation allowed the leadership to step away from heading up improvement efforts claiming that the program must gain momentum from the front-lines, and that projects should develop from the ground level – it is "their" program. However, without Leadership demonstrating commitment, setting direction, and "walking the walk", it was a lost cause at the front lines. This abdication of a leadership role led to confusion, false starts and increased cynicism among all employees.

Site 2 did attempt several other approaches skirting the full commitment we requested of the Leadership team. A front-line employee was put in charge of the CI program. Again, Leadership remained on the sidelines. This front-line colleague did a wonderful job by standardizing CI on-site. The initiative did begin to gain traction and benefits were experienced, but ultimately, the front-line employee could only request so much from his colleagues. Eventually, a steering group was formed to support the front-line colleague with team members from every function – *except Leadership*. The program again leapt forward with improvements realized in every department. The Committee had been provided no authority and in time members became frustrated – they also could only move the needle so far.

Over time, certain Leadership positions changed, ownership by the front-line teams grew and responsibilities for continuous improvement became a part of the job. Site 2 continues to try and close the gap between the two sites.

ENGAGEMENT

☑ CUSTOMER SATISFACTION   ☑ PRODUCTIVITY

☑ SAFETY   ☑ PROFITABILITY

☑ EMPLOYEE RETENTION   ☑ PROBLEM SOLVING

Engagement: the commitment and involvement an employee has with their organization and its goals.

"The unyielding truth is that people want to work in an organization where they are respected, valued and engaged. Create that culture and you will tap the unlimited potential that colleague engagement has to offer."

— Unknown

The Why

The engagement of workplace members is the most dynamic and potent resource available to all organizations today! It stands apart as a "game-changer" that could make a huge difference in performance and profitability and extensive research proves this out.

Well-respected research firms like Blessing White, Deloitte, Gallup and many others conclude that most core business measures such as productivity, profitability, safety incidents, customer satisfaction, quality, employee retention, and absenteeism are *all positively impacted by higher levels of employee engagement.*

The Power of Engagement

Gallup's polling demonstrates that the actual impact on these key measures is not marginal but *huge* and demonstrates how dramatic an impact "engagement" actually can be.

Gallup compiled 263 research studies across 192 organizations in 49 industries and 34 countries. Within each study, Gallup researchers statistically calculated the work-unit-level relationship between employee engagement and performance outcomes that the organization supplied. Researchers studied 49,928 work units, including nearly 1.4 million employees. This eighth iteration of the meta-analysis further confirmed the well-established connection between employee engagement and nine performance outcomes.[30]

Gallup measures engagement through actionable workplace elements with proven linkages to performance outcomes - opportunities for workers to do what they do best, opportunities to develop their job skills, and having their opinions count.[31]

Why a High-Engagement Culture Matters

According to Gallup, "a highly engaged workforce means the difference between a company that outperforms its competitors

30   Susan Sorenson. Gallup. How Employee Engagement Drives Growth. 2013. gallup.com/workplace/236927/employee - engagement - drives - growth.aspx

31   Jim Harter. Employee Engagement on the Rise in U.S. Gallup. August, 2018. news.gallup.com/poll/241649employee-engagement-rise.aspx

and one that fails to grow. It is a matter of life or death for a business."

Organizations and teams with higher employee engagement and lower active disengagement perform at higher levels. For example, organizations that are the best in engaging their employees achieve earnings-per-share growth that is more than four times that of their competitors.[32]

Engagement effect on Key Performance Indicators:

▶ Productivity: 17% higher

▶ Profitability: 21% higher

▶ Sales: 20% higher

▶ Shrinkage (theft): 28% lower

▶ Safety incidents: 70% lower

▶ Patient safety incidents:58% lower

▶ Customer metrics: 10% higher

▶ Defects: 40% lower

▶ Employee turnover: 24% - 59% lower

▶ Absenteeism: 41% lower

*median outcomes between top and bottom quartile work units

Gallup's polling is supported by the additional research by Deloitte indicating that 78% of corporate leaders say employee engagement is both an "urgent and important priority." Companies want continuous improvement and their employees can be the main drivers.

---

32   Ibid.

Contrast today's thinking with that of business leaders a decade or so ago. Many leaders then dismissed the notion that there are clear links between employee engagement and the organization's KPIs and overall success. That unfounded wisdom of old, still prevalent in many organizations, continues as these organizations still focus their attention primarily on process and very little on people. And those organizations continue to pay the price.

Understanding the Challenge

So, if the engagement of the workforce is truly "urgent and important" with business leaders agreeing that this huge valuable resource sits there largely untapped, then why do we continue to find that, over the last several decades, that a company's most unique asset, its employees, are disengaged in their work at a rate averaging 70%?[33]

2023 Gallup Workplace Report on

Employee Engagement

Engaged Employees: 32% These workers are involved in and enthusiastic about their work and workplace.

Not Engaged: 50% These workers are getting some of their workplace needs met but not very many. They tend to show up to work to do the minimum required and not much else.

---

33   Steve Crabtree. *Gallup World*. October, 2013.
      https://news.gallup.com/poll/165269/worldwide-employees-
      engaged-work.aspx

Actively Disengaged: 18% These employees are <u>disgruntled and disloyal because most of their workplace needs are unmet.</u>

In total, that means **68% <u>of the U.S. workforce is not engaged at work</u>**. This decline in engagement comes after a peak during the early stages of the pandemic when organizations demonstrated increased flexibility and empathy. <u>Unfortunately, since then, engagement has dropped significantly.</u>

So, What's The Problem

We believe the #1 reason for the high rate of disengaged employees is directly linked to *the traditional management formula.* Unlike their father's generation when employees felt fortunate to just have a job, this current workforce is no longer satisfied with their employment simply meeting basic financial needs. Today's workers seek more engagement, participation, recognition and personal growth. Based on research and decades of experience we hold that for businesses today: *the "traditional" model of leadership, as generally practiced, no longer works.*

In this chapter we will examine:

▶ Traditional Management and the Changing World

▶ Combining Wisdom and Experience

▶ Changing the Leadership Paradigm

▶ Training

▶ Systems Tweaking

▶ Expectations and Accountability

Traditional Management Formula

The traditional management system emerged during the industrial revolution and was heavy influenced by the military's "command and control" philosophy. This military style of leadership was further entrenched by the work of theorists like Fredrick Winslow Taylor. Taylor had studied mechanical engineering and conducted time and motion studies searching for ways to boost productivity. In 1909 Taylor, published management practices that would be known as "The Principles of Scientific Management". First deployed in factories in Philadelphia, this approach to managing quickly spread. Best known is the deployment of Scientific Management by Henry Ford in the massive Ford Rouge Plant in Detroit.

Taylor advocated that jobs be simplified and standardized and workers be assigned based on their capabilities and motivation. He believed that money was the sole motivator and the supervisor's job was to monitor workers performance to ensure efficiency. Taylor also advocated that managers should devote their time to planning and solving problems.

Over the decades, other theorists contributed to the evolution of what we know today as Traditional Management Practices. And, for better or for worse, these guideposts continue to define management's role in most organizations.

The list below identifies some of the distinguishing characteristics of the Traditional Management philosophy negatively impacting employee engagement:

▶ Positions of authority demand respect and compliance.

▶ Control the workforce – enforce rules.

▶ Information is limited and controlled.

▶ Control all resource allocation.

- ▶ Decisions are made top-down.

- ▶ Management solves problems.

- ▶ Generates improvement ideas.

- ▶ Determines roles and responsibilities.

Although these practices are not likely to be found in the company manual, in reality, they aptly reflect the criteria by which many manager's/supervisor's performance are actually measured. These and other features of traditional management bind leaders to adherence and their performance is judged on how well they carry out these functions. Recognize too that most organization's leaders have been chosen and promoted based upon these criteria.

Changing World

The world has shifted dramatically over the decades, while many management practices in general, have not. Global competition, new technology, changing demographics, customer demands, employee satisfaction and retention, legal and environmental requirements, cultural and societal norms, virtually all of these factors, that shape business strategy today have experienced significant change. Yet, many organizations if not most still cling to those management tenets of a bygone era. Recognize also that most organizations are locked in this cycle of tradition. Tradition provides a level of certainty and predictability. Is it any wonder that establishing a collaborative environment, where front-line employees are encouraged to provide input and help solve problems, struggle to gain traction?

Management's Uncertain Role

A second major reason for the lack of traction for employee engagement efforts in organizations is, as it has been for decades, directly linked to the ambiguity of the new roles and responsibilities for current management leaders. While the expanding role for rank and file frontline members is generally well defined, the roles and responsibilities that management would assume seem vague and increasingly unclear. Talk of becoming a "coach", "team liaison" and "mentor" create uncertainty, as few actually know what these terms even mean. This lack of clarity contributes to the normal resistance to change through the management ranks, especially the frontline management with the most at stake. Facing a loss of identity, it is no surprise that passive resistance continues to rule the day.

This resistance and uncertainty are unfortunate, as the *role and need for competent frontline management has actually expanded with the engagement of the rank and file.*

Combining Wisdom and Experience

Because the engagement of employees reflects a significant change in culture, implementation takes time, serious commitment and strong leaders to make it viable. This is not a plug and play effort where the implementation path is straightforward and predictable. Knowing that the requisites of good managerial performance had been forged over the last century helps explain why so many in the management ranks can't believe that the organization's leaders actually want them to share their key responsibilities with their non-managerial staff. For decades, very competent management employees have been required to lead the charge, make the good decisions, and keep the troops in line. If they did it well, they were rewarded, and if they did not, they were chastised.

What ties us in knots is that *employee engagement does not, in any way, suggest that managers are no longer in charge.* Management is still responsible for running the organization, making the right decisions, planning effectively, staffing efficiently, solving problems etc. No advocate for employee participation is suggesting that management should vacate these traditional roles and responsibilities. In fact, employee engagement requires managers to assume additional roles in supporting the frontlines.

What advocates do say is that *frontline colleagues also have experience, knowledge and expertise and should be allowed and encouraged to contribute.* It stands to reason that together, combining the wisdom and experience of all members, organizations are better able to meet the significant challenges they now confront.

Successful implementation requires a fundamental change in the thinking and behaviors of managers, supervisors and the frontlines. In order for this change to get traction, employees of all stripes need a clear understanding of what their future role entails and a compelling reason why the change is necessary.

Changing the leadership paradigm employee engagement requires strong leadership – and strong leaders demand answers. If the goal is to shift from the traditional management philosophy to one that fosters employee participation, then managers and supervisors need to know why! And, they must be onboard. If these leaders are not with you, they will forestall your efforts, either consciously or unconsciously at every turn.

Providing statistics can help. Sharing the positive impact that engagement has on key performance indicators also assists in making the business case. Additionally, sharing other measures such as higher employee retention, greater job satisfaction, lower absenteeism, and fewer safety incidents also further demonstrates the long-term benefits to both the organization and its members.

Seasoned managers and supervisors however, are justifiably skeptical of the introduction of yet a new undertaking; especially change that has immediate impact on them and their future. Your leadership group has likely seen programs come and go, some stuck many have not. Yet, the command and control management philosophy has remained pretty much intact, in good times and bad, managers were rewarded for doing it well. Challenging this mindset, reinforced for generations, does not come easy.

But there is good news: Employees — both managerial and front-line — are open to greater participation and engagement. Most members DESIRE a role in helping their organization achieve its goals - but they don't want to be made a fool.

Changing the Paradigm Begins With Communication

Like all well-constructed improvement efforts, taking the time to develop a comprehensive communication strategy is all-important. Employees throughout your organization will be impacted by this shift so they need to know what is happening and how they can support the effort. Always keep in mind that any change that challenges the status-quo will likely generate a level of fear among your colleagues. Recognize too, that these fears are legitimate and develop your communications with their concerns in mind. Respond to questions before they are even asked. Let colleagues know what is going to happen, what will be expected of them, any training that will be provided, and other factors that will support the effort. Use traditional and non-traditional forms of communication to reach out. Face-to-face, written communications, group meetings, and newsletters all contribute to a well-constructed plan.

Above all, MAKE IT SAFE.

Patience is a Virtue

Visiting a client site recently, I had the opportunity to spend some time alone in the team meeting area. Before long, I was absorbed in the team's visual management charts. This three-year-old team met daily to discuss their performance from the previous day and address any major issues that kept them from meeting their goals. Totally absorbed, with my nose about three inches from the boards, I eventually became aware of Charlie, the CI site leader standing next to me laughing. I was puzzled and asked: "what's so darn funny?" Charlie explained that just last week, he saw Stan, a hard-nosed machine operator, holding the same pose as me, with his nose just three inches from the charts! This seemed remarkable as my clear memory of Stan was that of an excellent machine operator, who had absolutely no interest in participating in improvement efforts and was considered by his peers- "the leader of the resistance". Charlie recounted, that during the first year of the CI efforts, the entire team would resist participating in the daily meetings, staring blankly at the charts and listening little to what the team leader had to say. Led by Stan, this group more closely resembled a biker gang than an engaged group of machine operators.

Now here it was two years later that Stan, the "Leader of the Resistance", had tackled a long-standing machining problem. He, along with others on his team, had done some problem solving and come up with a low cost, mistake proofing tool to reduce scrap, minimize downtime and made the operator's job easier. On the team's visual management board, was a list of actions and deadlines. The action list indicated that the tool would be built and available by this specific day – it wasn't and Stan was angry.

Charlie, sporting a huge smile, went on to explain that the team meeting had ended 10 minutes before and Stan insisted that he would not begin work until the action board was updated with the actual status of the improvement tool. Stan wanted confirmation that Maintenance was at least moving forward with the prototype. Within minutes, the board was updated, the tool was nearly finished and would be available within 24 hours - Stan went back to work. The following day, Stan and his team had the tool, and it turned out to be a significant improvement across the machining operation.

Three years into the process, the Supervisor no longer facilitates the team meeting. Machine Operators rotate through that that role on a monthly basis. Team boards are up to date, engagement is obvious and powerful!

During my visit to this site, I was again reminded that engaging employees in improvements efforts is not a straight forward path. Each initiative is unique, people and organizational cultures differ. Many might have thrown in the towel with this front-line team, citing the resistance from Stan and his workmates. But Charlie never gave up. He was committed, he was patient and eventually it paid off!

Changing Paradigms Takes Time

You can't expect a supervisor, who has been rewarded and promoted for their ability to kick butt and take names, to readily adopt a new approach to leading. They need to understand this effort is important and a key aspect of your organization's strategy. It also should be made clear that their participation and support is needed and required.

Your current management group, whether hired to those positions or promoted from within, all possess certain managerial and/or technical abilities and skills. It is highly unlikely however, that any were hired specifically for their ability to engage their colleagues. This new challenge of welcoming participation and actively seeking input and fresh ideas from their front-line colleagues may fly in the face of their past experiences and how they see themselves and their jobs duties. Enforcing rules and making decisions is what they have been paid to do. They need clarity now as to what exactly are the new expectations and what are their job responsibilities.

Managers and supervisors are always on the front line of change efforts. Their positions are usually the most challenging and often, the least rewarded in an organization. *This group needs support and deserves training.* If your organization is like many that we work with, the training and coaching of managers and supervisors has not been a high priority. And yet, this group likely has the greatest impact on the operational bottom line – go figure?

"Supervisors, if carefully selected, well-trained, highly motivated and given the status and pay appropriate to being the 'professional at managing the processes and people' can make more difference to the long-term success of the organization than any group other than top management. And even here it is the supervisor who delivers top management's policies in the workplace." [34]

—Peter Wickens

If your leadership team cannot be convinced of the need to make this change – it will not happen! Your management group must be clear on if and how their duties will change and what behaviors are expected of them. Providing training and coaching can also help the transition.

Basic Management Training

Providing your management team with some basic training will also help reduce resistance, while instilling a level of confidence in those now charged with the meaningful engagement of others. Skills and training managers and supervisors usually find helpful include:

▶ Safety first

▶ Leading change

▶ Communications (listening, giving, and receiving feedback)

---

34 Peter Wickens. *The Ascendant Organization*. (London: Palgrave MacMillian 1995.)

▶ Collaborative leadership, delegation and accountability

▶ Team dynamics and empowerment

▶ Problem solving

▶ Decision making

▶ Managing differences

▶ Effective interaction and diversity

Time for an Anecdote

A CFO asks the CEO: "What happens if we invest in developing our people and then they leave us?"

The CEO responds: "What happens if we don't and they stay?"

Front-line Team Member Training

Corresponding training for the front-liners is also an integral step in creating the environment where employees can contribute. Training may include:

▶ Safety first

▶ Team roles and responsibility

▶ Team metrics

▶ Problem solving

▶ Improvement generation and implementation

Leading by Example

Leaders across the organization, from the executive level to the front line, must "walk the talk," encouraging and facilitating engagement whenever feasible. All managerial staff must understand that engaging employees is not an option but a key component of your organization's business strategy.

Figure 3: The área leader and team members discuss options.

Developing a culture that values and listens to its employees takes time, patience, and commitment. All eyes will be on the organization's leaders as the front line and managerial group seek to determine if this "employee engagement" is for real or just the latest fad.

Front-line employees will quickly recognize whether their supervisor is sincere or simply going through the motions. If their efforts are real, most front-liners will appreciate the greater inclusion, trust, and participation in the business.

Systems Support

Organizations readily embark on efforts to increase employee involvement and participation, often forgetting that the organization's systems will need to be tweaked in order to support this change. Regardless of how effective conveying the importance and positive impact of engaging employees may have been, if systems do not adapt to accommodate and support this effort, sustainability may remain elusive.

For example: shared information is the lifeblood of most organizations and yet one of the most challenging to get right. The importance of communicating in an environment of employee engagement becomes even more critical. Vital information must be shared to enable non-managerial staff to become part of something broader than just meeting daily requirements.[35]

If communications are poor, people feel "out of the loop" and view this as confirmation that they are not really trusted and that this engagement stuff is just window dressing. The communication system is but one element that can support and anchor your engagement initiatives.

Think of integrating other departments such as Safety, Quality, Operations, Maintenance, Sales, Customer Services etc., into sharing information and seeking input from the front-liners, further demonstrating the value and opportunity that engagement provides.

Your Human Resource department can add further weight to the legitimacy and long-term commitment by realigning their current systems of promotions, compensation, employee evaluations, and hiring to reflect new behaviors deemed important.

---

35 William Neher. *Organizational Communications: Challenges of Change, Diversity and Continuity.* (Boston: Allyn & Bacon 1997).

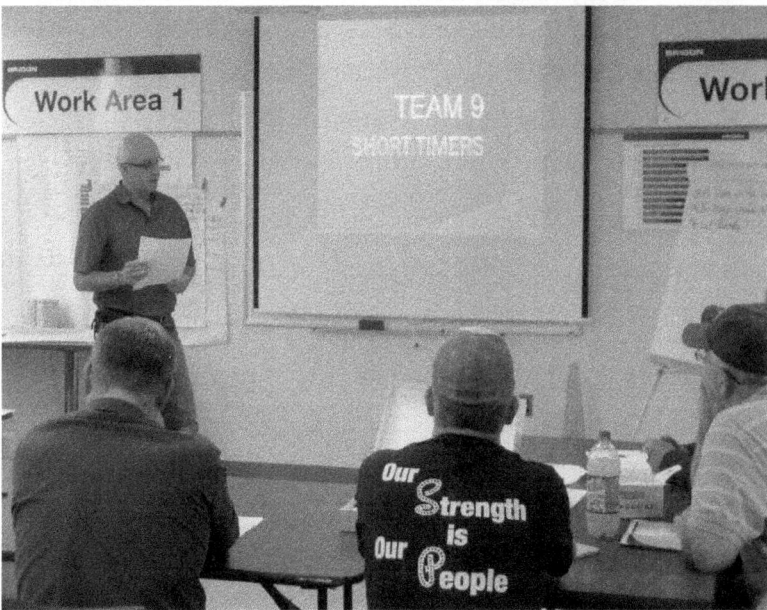

Figure 4: Colleagues in training.

Establish a Steering Group

An effective way to increase participation, build momentum, and help bridge the communication chasm is through the formation of a steering group. A steering group typically provides strategic direction and guidance that supports the program's objectives and the project leaders. By including key members of your organization in the steering group, you expand commitment and ownership of the initiative, broaden responsibility for success, establish a communication network, increase accountability and thereby expand employee involvement.

While each steering group may differ somewhat, the role often includes:

▶ Leading and guiding the change effort.

▶ Communicating continuously.

▶ Overseeing, monitoring and guiding employee participation in the effort.

▶ Identifying and attacking underlying organizational issues preventing increased performance and participation.

▶ Educating themselves and others in the process.

▶ Approving and enabling the implementation of recommendations and policies.

▶ Defining and communicating the case for change – THE WHY.

▶ Defining outcomes, boundaries, measurements, and timelines for the change initiative.

▶ Reviewing progress toward outcomes.

▶ Modeling the new behaviors that reflect the changes – "walk the talk."

▶ Setting the values and accompanying behaviors that shape the culture.

▶ Approving and overseeing the project plan for the change process.

▶ Coordinating all major activities relating to the improvement effort.

▶ Ensuring that all CI efforts support the overall organization's strategy.

Identifying Key Members of a CI Steering Group

▶ Seek those who have had experience with improvement efforts in their careers.

▶ Identify key leaders (no matter their title) who may influence engagement and provide inspiration.

▶ Draw on the strengths of others who may carry the torch of a new initiative.

▶ Seek representatives from every aspect of the business.

Continuous Improvement Leaders run the risk of having their efforts perceived as "their program." Depending on the existing culture; actions, audits, and progress may be perceived as the sole responsibility of this representative or the CI department. Steering groups help to shift this perspective, create a "we" culture and distribute the necessary actions and responsibilities throughout the organization.

Other benefits of a steering group may be:

▶ Insight from each department is shared – different levels of the organization inform next steps.

▶ An informal channel of feedback regarding the initiative is created.

▶ Pitfalls are avoided.

▶ An opportunity to continually communicate is established.

Start with a Charter

Creating a charter for and with the steering group is an important step to ensure that each member understands their role and responsibilities and is willing to lend time and support to the effort.

The purpose of a charter is to clarify the group's purpose, members, boundaries, roles and responsibilities, resources and duration. We recommend that a charter is developed together with its members in a group session. By doing so, understanding and commitment is created and individuals become aware of expectations. By spending time at its inception, team members develop ownership, avoid confusion, and can organize themselves in an efficient manner.

Purpose of the Steering Group:

_____

_____

Rationale (Why This Effort Is Important):

_____

_____

Goals/Objectives/Measures Of Success:

_____

_____

Team Members:

_____

_____

Key Issues To Be Addressed:

_____

_____

Boundaries & Constraints:

_____

_____

Reporting Responsibility:

_____

_____

Resources Available:

_____

_____

Roles Needed (Who?):

_____

_____

Subgroups Required:

_____

_____

Duration (Length Of Service Required) (To Be Disbanded By?):

Other:

Shared Responsibilities via Steering Group

One particular client of ours was a small manufacturing plant. The CI representative was chosen because of their role in the Quality Department. A pleasant demeanor and through understanding of metrics and root cause analysis made them the obvious choice for the initiative. Establishing a separate CI department did not make sense for this particular site.

As consultants, we provided training and the launch of the CI program and initial benefits were observed by all. It became apparent after six months that the low-hanging fruit had been picked and an obvious plateau to the program had arrived. Much of the early inertia was waning and actions and recommendations lingered for months.

A conversation with the Quality/CI representative painted a stark picture. When asked why CI actions remained for months without progress, he remarked "Let me be blunt. I am first a Quality representative. That is why I was hired. If I miss a defect or sign-off on a responsibility, in our industry, I will be fired. I understand the importance of CI and I know it will help me with my role in Quality, but quality issues are here today. I don't get fired for pushing out CI deadlines. I am only one person."

We decided to create a steering group to support his efforts. Key representatives were chosen from every department. Responsibilities and actions were shared. The program was no longer perceived as "his project". Momentum picked back up and results continued to improve.

Clear Expectations and Accountability

As with other aspects of continuous improvement, expectations for management and staff need to be well communicated and understood. It follows that, once these behavioral expectations are established, shared accountability to these new norms is not optional but required.

Resistance will likely be encountered. However, once a strategy charted by those entrusted to lead an organization is adopted and adequately explained, it is time to move ahead.

The road up the mountain is never straight up, but all organization members — yes even the skeptics — need to understand the behaviors expected of them and how progress will be measured. Employees desire feedback. They wish to know how well they are doing and how their work impacts the overall results of the organization. Employees want and need goals and measures and the support necessary to achieve them. *(*Reference: Reward/Recognition in Accountability Chapter)*

Those who simply cannot or will not adapt to the chosen path, after training, coaching and reasonable time, need to relocate to another area of the organization or leave.

Final Word

Few of us, chosen to lead Continuous Improvement efforts, fail to see the value in enlisting the participation of others — in fact, we know in order to be successful – we must. Despite the fits and starts many organizations experience, research confirms and we already know, that employees long for the opportunity to contribute to the success of their organization. We have found that *people want to work in an organization where they are respected, valued and engaged. Create that culture and you will tap the unlimited potential that employee engagement has to offer.*

ENGAGEMENT TAKEAWAYS

► Engaging Employees stands alone as the one resource all organizations have that could make a huge difference in performance, profitability, and employee satisfaction.

► Only 30% of all workers are actively engaged at work.

► The legacy of "Traditional Management" remains the biggest barrier to Employee Engagement.

The Steering Group Charter template is available for download at www.thefivekeys.org

CASE STUDY: THE TWO SISTER SITES SOLVING THE PUZZLE

Engagement: the commitment and involvement an employee has with their organization and its goals.

Site 1's performance results did not excel during the first few years. Employee engagement also was slow to gain momentum. Not to say that they were underperforming, but like most other sites across this organization, employee engagement was yet another hill to climb. As the program matured and Leadership set the example, there was a steady growth in colleague participation in CI activities. Site 1 did not push for results, nor attempt to grow the program quickly – they were patient and made it a priority to focus on consistency and reliable systems to support engagement.

Systems such as a process to capture and implement team member ideas and a robust reward and recognition program encouraged employees to dip their toes in the water of a growing CI culture. Employees realized that this was a safe environment in which to problem-solve, to offer suggestions and try new things. And they were recognized for it!

As the program matured, and an understanding of CI grew, employees throughout the organization were identified and invited to join a steering group. Employees were chosen not for their position or rank, but by their strong leadership and commitment with the teams they represented. No longer was this a "CI program" – it was the way they did business.

Figure 5: The power of engagement!

It became apparent that there was a transformation underway here. While several other sites had started strong, Site 1 eventually surpassed the performance of others across the globe. Ten years later, Site 1 continues to maintain high levels of employee engagement in pursuit of continuous improvement. Several other sites that started strong no longer have a viable CI program or they have lost momentum in pursuing daily improvement opportunities. Focused on achieving immediate results rather than establishing a long-term CI culture was their undoing.

As Site 2 took a very hands-off approach to the CI initiative, some teams were still willing to test the waters – and did. Employees utilized the tools they had learned and solved problems, often coming up with novel solutions to address their issues. But ultimately, enthusiasm diminished as a desperately needed management process to escalate decision making and implement improvement suggestions went unanswered. Improvement suggestions were stalled and implementation support was lacking. Front-line employees became frustrated and unclear on how to meet expectations and slowly withdrew.

There was a second factor that contributed to low colleague engagement that surfaced as well. The "results-focused" culture continued to impede the CI process. Employees were reluctant to volunteer for activities that could possibly fail or not achieve the expected results. It was risky. For example, there was a perceived risk associated with being the bearer of bad news or attempting to solve a problem and failing. There was a fear of sticking your neck out. Reprimands and the perception of possible discipline hung heavy in the air. High rates of employee turnover pointed to the low morale at the site.

Finally, consistency in messaging also contributed to the challenge of building engagement at Site 2. After the frontline Steering Group was formed, there was hope this action would stimulate engagement and empower employees. In fact, this message even was communicated by the Leadership. However, when problems were experienced, management quickly took control of the situation. Employees were told how to respond and management was there to verify their direction. Even though these employees were told repeatedly that they knew their role better than anybody else and their ideas to improve were important to the process, they recognized that this was not what they experienced on the job. Employees quickly learned how to walk a fine line between messaging and actions. Employee engagement continued to suffer.

The difference in employee engagement between Site 1 and Site 2 is illustrated in this short story. Site 2 was experiencing some major start-up issues after an annual week-long plant shut-down. The shut-down had been scheduled in order to perform maintenance and make improvement modifications to the manufacturing process. However, this particular year, Site 2 struggled to bring equipment back on-line and meet specific product requirements. After three long days of continuing to struggle with the start-up, a few employees were brought over from Site 1 to support the effort and assist in making corrections. Site 1 managers, operators, and maintenance employees quickly problem solved, designed experiments, and identified solutions. Their efforts however, were questioned at every turn. Fear of failure was palatable and solutions were discounted. After a 16-hour day working in a somewhat hostile, unfamiliar, and unempowered environment; morale among the Site 1 team had evaporated and they were defeated. The goal of solving the problem was overshadowed by the lack of help they could provide in this environment. They packed up at 1 a.m. and made the long drive home. Site 2 took three more days to come back on-line - eventually using the guidelines established during that miserable 16-hour day.

GOAL ALIGNMENT

Goal Alignment: the process of aligning individual employee goals with the strategic goals of the organization, creating a direct line of sight which connects all members to a common purpose and plan.

"If you don't know where you are going, any road will get you there."

— Lewis Carroll,
English writer of *Alice's Adventure in Wonderland*

In today's competitive business environment, organizations of all stripes require the wisdom, experience, and participation of all their employees. And, most employees truly wish to contribute to the success of their organizations, to be part of something bigger, and to make a difference. But in order to contribute in this way, employees must know and understand where their organization is headed and what are the expectations for them. *The necessity of linking the organization's vision and strategic goals to the daily performance of front-line employees is vital.*

Converting and aligning a complex multi-year business strategy to the daily work practices and measures of front-line employees is the ultimate challenge. Multiple studies show that providing meaningful goals that employees can rally behind, directly impact, and feel invested in improves the quality and quantity of those employee's work. Furthermore, it is a top motivator for employee engagement.

The Challenge

"Only 14% of employees understand their company's strategy."

—William Schiemann[36]

When we came across the result of the study quoted above, we were more than a little skeptical. How could it be that the overwhelming majority of employees in organizations throughout North America did not really know the strategy and goals of their company? How could it be possible, in a world of global competitiveness and instant communications, that something so central to running a successful enterprise would not be understood by the people who do the work?

Being responsible skeptics, we did some more digging and found an equally disturbing article in the *Harvard Business Review* by John Kotter.[37] Kotter informs us that, even in high-performing companies with "clearly articulated public strategies," only 29% of employees recognize and correctly identify their company's strategy *when given six choices!*

---

36 James W. Smither and Manuel London. *Performance Management: Putting Research Into Action.* (SanFrancisco: Josey-Bass, 2009).

37 John Kotter. "When CEOs Talk Strategy, Is Anyone Listening?" *Harvard Business Review.* 2013.

Even using the most generous analysis of the existing research, only 30% of employees actually know and understand their organization's strategy. But let's assume that these statistics are really off the mark. Rather than 3 of 10, let's double that number and give credit to 6 of 10 employees for knowing their company's strategy — fair enough? That leaves 4 of 10, or fully 40%, of the North American workforce that don't. Consider the negative impact and misalignment to achieving your organization's objectives. How can leaders expect to achieve their vision, strategy, and goals when almost half of the organization doesn't even know what they are? Answer: They can't!

Surprised by the answers??????

For those of you that doubt these studies, try it yourself.

Ask colleagues to describe your organization's strategy.

Can they? Can you?

The Gauntlet

The critical challenge for every organization is linking the organization's strategy to the daily actions of each member, and this can be the most powerful and motivating linchpin in your business strategy. Identifying daily goals and measures provides colleagues with an understanding of what is needed by their organization and how they can contribute from their work stations. Additionally, the appropriate goals and measures will focus members on specific behaviors that shift culture to one that drives specific results.

In this chapter we focus on five aspects of Goal Alignment to meet the alignment challenges in your organization:

- ▶ The Power of Vision

- ▶ Strategy Development and Deployment using OGSM Model

- ▶ Communicating the Plan – The Elevator Speech

- ▶ Goal Alignment Using a KPI grid

- ▶ Visual Management of Goals and Measures

Vision acts as a "North Star" and is the catalyst from which goals, strategies, and measures are identified. Unlike goals, strategies and measures, <u>a vision remains constant and does not change.</u>

A vision statement describes a future state that an organization seeks to achieve. Often, a vision statement applies to an entire organization but can also apply to a single activity or a single department. Regardless of its scope, a vision describes a picture of where you wish to be in the future.

The Power of Vision

In our view, an effective vision statement underpins three critical aspects of a continuous improvement initiative.

- ▶ **The vision commits the leadership team to a path for change.** By creating a "vision," top leadership is admitting and committing to their employees that the status quo is not sustainable and that a different course must be charted.

- ▶ **Leadership's commitment sparks additional support.** Once the "vision" is adopted and communicated, alignment in support of the vision begins to take place. Secondary leaders, throughout the enterprise, are now on notice that this initiative — whatever it happens to be — is to be supported. Support can come in many forms, but throughout the organization, members now are aware that they are expected to support and advance this drive for change.

▶ **A vision provides the basis for 'goal alignment' through the development of strategies and measures.** Without specific goals, strategies, and measures being set forth, real progress is unlikely. A vision provides a vivid image of an end-state, what we strive to accomplish.

Creating a Meaningful Vision Statement

An effective vision statement should speak to colleagues as well as customers and stakeholders. It should be: **informative, inspiring, and simple.**

For example, the focus of the fictitious Able Products Company, (currently rated #4 in quality), was to become #1 in quality among their business competitors. The leadership team worked together to draft this vision statement: **Able Products Company is known as: The #1 Solutions-Based Quality Leader.**

Strategy Development – Creating a Roadmap – Include Others

Now that Able Products has articulated a clear and compelling vision, they now need a strategy and roadmap to get there. Often, we look to executive leadership to provide this plan, but it may fall to you as the CI leader to be part of its development.

Experience has taught us that including leaders from across the various functions and departments in that development will build support for the project and yourself, while avoiding needless mistakes and reboots.

Building on the vision statement, the Able leadership team agreed the following strategy: **Within the next 18 months, establish a problem-solving culture, teaching colleagues to identify and solve quality issues and implement solutions.**

Creating a Roadmap

The next step is to develop a comprehensive plan that colleagues will understand, appreciate, and support. In this example, we utilize the well-known OGSM planning model: Objectives, Goals, Strategies, Measures.

OGSM Planning Model

The comprehensive OGSM planning model has four main aspects:

1. **Objectives:** Broad thrusts where the organization must make significant improvements in the next 3-5 years.

2. **Goals:** Achievable and measurable results in the next 1-2 years.

3. **Strategies / Actions:**

   - What will we do?

   - Who will do it?

   - How is it to be done?

4. **Measures:**

   - Specific timelines and milestones

   - Resources required

   - Visual Department KPI Charts

Vision: Able Products Company is known as: The #1 Solutions-Based Quality Leader.

Strategy: Within the next 18 months, establish a problem-solving culture, teaching colleagues to identify and solve quality issues and implement solutions.

OGSM Model for Strategy Deployment
Able Products Company

OBJECTIVES	GOALS	STRATEGIES	MEASURES
Broad thrusts 3 to 5 yrs.	Achievable results 1 to 2 yrs.	How will we achieve our objectives? Processes, Programs, Initiatives, Systems	How will we know we are successful?
"Quality is Job 1". Eliminate customer complaints. Become known as "The Solutions Based" Industry Quality Leader.	Train all employees in basic problem-solving techniques by December 20YY. Improve the Defect Rate by 2% each month. Reduce customer complaints by 50% within 12 months.	Communicate to all stakeholders our Vision	Letters to Key Stakeholders All Hands Meeting Signs, Handouts, Promos
		Train and engage all employees in Basic Problem Solving	Colleagues trained Problems addressed Solutions implemented
		Launch: Time-to-Detect, Time-to-Correct Learning Cycle Quality System	Hourly, Daily, Weekly & Monthly defect rates
		Become the most responsive customer complaint organization	Hours between a customer complaint and remedy

A comprehensive strategy translates an abstract vision into a concrete and tangible plan of action. A plan that can be communicated, understood, and measured.

Communicating the Plan

The research demonstrates that successful change initiatives are supported by an effective communication plan. Ideally, every member of your organization knows and understands the vision, the goals, and strategies necessary to make the vision a reality and, most importantly, their role in helping achieve these goals.

In communicating the roadmap, don't overwhelm your colleagues:(1) Make it safe, so members are not fearful of the endeavor or their ability to contribute and (2) Keep it simple and focused. More on communications is found in the Leadership chapter.

Key Performance Indicators: Aligning Goals Throughout the Organization

Key Performance Indicators (KPIs) are measurements that demonstrate how effectively a company or department is performing. Organizations use KPIs to evaluate their success in pursuit of their goals.

As the continuous improvement roadmap is launched, identifying and communicating the corresponding KPIs in each area/department becomes the next step in the process. To be effective, a KPI should be:

▶ Aligned and contribute to the strategy, goals, and customer requirements.

▶ Quantifiable and simple.

▶ Well-communicated and understood.

▶ Measures that members can influence.

There are thousands of possible KPIs depending on the type of business or process that an organization is assessing. For the Able Products example, four common KPI categories demonstrate how this could work for you: Quality, Throughput, Cost-effectiveness and People

Building a KPI Grid

Keeping this to basics, let's assume that at the Able Products Company there is one level of management and just four departments: production, quality, shipping and maintenance.

In this scenario, the same four KPI categories (Quality, Throughput, Cost-effectiveness and Safety/People) will have different measures for each department - yet each measure aligns with the vision, goals, and strategy.

In the grid below, you can see how these measures differ and yet are aligned throughout the organization.

Able's Vision: To be known as "The Solutions-Based Quality Leader."

Able's Strategy: Within the next 18 months, establish a problem-solving culture, teaching colleagues to identify and solve quality issues and implement solutions.

By aligning these four KPI categories in each department, goals and measures can now be developed establishing a comprehensive goal alignment system.

Setting Goals:

▶ When setting goals, ensure that goals are aligned with the <u>vision, strategy and customer requirements.</u>

▶ Goals should be <u>achievable</u>

▶ Goals and targets should <u>support desired behaviors.</u>

For example:

Teams	Management Team	Operations Team	Shipping Team	Quality Team	Maintenance Team
When/ Where Meeting Times	Daily 9:30-10:00 Training Room	Daily 10 minute meeting each shift 8 a.m. / 4 p.m. / 12 a.m.	Daily 10 minute meeting each shift 8 a.m./ 8 p.m. Room D	Daily 10 minute meeting each shift 8 a.m. Lab Office	Weekly Fridays 7:30 a.m. to 8 a.m. TBD
Who Meeting Participants	All Managers and Team Leaders #2 shift	Team Members Supervisor	Team Members Team Leader	Team Members Supervisor (Team Leader)	All Maintenance Team Members / Supervisors
Quality	**Measure:** Customer Complaints Goal: Reduce customer complaints by 50% in 12 months	**Measure:** Off-spec by machine by shift Goal: Increase "to spec" parts from 94% to 98% in 12 months	**Measure:** Glue issues per case codes Goal: Reduce glue issues by 10% in 12 months – take action on every occurrence	**Measure:** Internal and External complaints. Goal: Increase from 90 to 100% accuracy of daily self-audits (second point of inspection)	**Measure:** Equipment failures Goal: 80% preventative / 20% corrective Improve from 68% to 80% in 12 months
Speed / Throughput	**Measure:** Increase volume Goal: Improve efficiency by 15% in 12 months	**Measure:** Adherence to production plan Goal: Reduce deviations from plan by 50% in 12 months	**Measure:** Cases / hour Goal: 100% attainment of shipping schedule	**Measure:** Adherence to inspection schedule Goal: 100% daily audit completion	**Measure:** Downtime hours / number of repeat failures Goal: Reduce repeat failures by 50% by 3rd quarter

Teams	Management Team	Operations Team	Shipping Team	Quality Team	Maintenance Team
Cost Effective- ness	**Measure:** Complaint response time Goal: Respond within 24 hours	**Measure:** Rework Goal: Reduce rework by 40% in 12 months	**Measure:** Shipping damage Goal: Reduce shipping damage by 20% - take action on each occurrence	**Measure:** Number of cases rejected Goal: 10% improvement on Time to Detect / Time to Correct within 6 months.	**Measure:** Planned maintenance completion Goal: 100% weekly completion
People	**Measure:** Compliance to problem-solving training Goal: Train all members in basic problem-solving within six months.	**Measure:** Number of improvement ideas submitted / implemented Goal: Implement 3 improvements per shift every month – 100% adherence to monthly training schedule	**Measure:** Number of improvements submitted / implemented Goal: Implement 3 improvement suggestions every month - 100% adherence to monthly training schedule	**Measure:** Number of improvements submitted / implemented Goal: Implement 3 improvement suggestions every month - 100% adherence to monthly training schedule	**Measure:** Number of implemented improvements each week Goal: Reduce the backlog of improvement implementatio ns by 50% in 6 months. 100% adherence to monthly safety and problem-solving training schedule

*The KPI Grid is not confined to manufacturing. We have deployed similar alignment strategies in service organizations such as, banks, hospitals and administrative support within manufacturing organizations.

As you can see in this grid, goals have been developed for each KPI (Quality, Speed/Throughput, Cost-effectiveness, People) and each department (Management, Production, Shipping, Quality and Maintenance). With these clear goals, strategies and measures now established, both leadership and front-line colleagues clearly understand expectations and effectively manage their contribution to the business.

"The most empowering condition of all is when the entire organization is aligned with its mission, and people's passions and purpose are in synch with each other."

—Bill George, Professor of Management Practice, Harvard Business School, former CEO Medtronic

How Is Success In Your Organization Determined?

Maybe the pollsters are right after all. Maybe employees don't really understand their organization's strategy or how they can contribute to their organization's success. This phenomenon, we learned firsthand, is not confined to front-line employees. Recently, when working with a management group at a well-known company with locations scattered around the globe, we encountered equally surprising testimonials. Our work with this corporate group focused on establishing a continuous improvement effort designed to engage the employees in streamlining their work processes and improving customer satisfaction.

During the very first meeting on our first day of work with the business leader and a dozen department managers, we simply asked them how their company function was measured? What are their criteria for success? Following a long uncomfortable pause, where the department managers looked to each other and the business leader for clues, came the honest truth: they really didn't know! They worked very hard, each of the dozen departments, staffed by professionals, working diligently to get the work out, but were unsure as to how their efforts were viewed and if there actually were measures at all.

Needless to say, the development of vision, strategy, goals, and measures were now at the top of their to-do list.

Visual Management

Visual management is perhaps the most effective way to share information and create an energized workplace. There are a variety of visual charts and graphs available to complement your visual management of KPIs. <u>The objective is to:</u>

1. Visually capture each department's performance.

2. Review performance on a daily basis.

3. Establish a clear line of sight between the vision, goals and measures and the work people are doing each day.

Each goal and measure that has been defined can be made visible by choosing from many visual control options (i.e., color coding, visual performance boards, signage, shadow boards, floor demarcation) best suited to your specific measure.

The purpose of visual management is insight, not numbers. Visual management allows you to instantly compare expected performance to the actual and take action when performance is not acceptable. Implemented correctly, visual management promotes ownership, focus, transparency, problem-solving, and thus, encourages continuous improvement.

A Common Dilemma

When we begin working with front-line teams, we often pose the question "did you have a good day on the job yesterday?" Almost without exception, you quickly hear that "yes, we had a good day - things went well." We follow that up with another question, "how do you know?" Now things get a bit quiet, responses often range from "we think we had a good day, we didn't hear any complaints" or "our boss didn't yell at us" and on it goes with no real criteria to support their claim of having a good day.

Here you have a group of good employees who could provide a minute-by-minute recap of yesterday's ballgame, who scored first, who was pitching, the final score, etc. But when it came to their work, where they spent at least 8 hours, they could not definitively demonstrate with evidence that they had a good day! Try this sometime and see what you find.

Advantages of Visual Management

▶ Provides instant feedback.

▶ Measurement is the base for improvement.

▶ The scoreboard motivates and inspires.

▶ A scoreboard focuses people on what is important.

▶ When assistance is required, it becomes apparent.

▶ Trends and performance gaps become clear, generating quick remedial actions.

▶ Visual management allows every member to know and understand how they are performing, highlights trends, and triggers problem-solving. This insight encourages members to be proactive and accountable.

Shorten Feedback Time

Visual Management must be *relevant* and *up to date*. If expected performance does not match actual performance, current feedback allows quick and immediate actions. To review the week's performance failures on a Friday afternoon is practically worthless. The week is over, the run is complete, the rejects are already counted. IT'S TOO LATE!!!

The distinction between monitoring performance and managing performance is important to note. When managing performance, corrective action taken on a daily basis based on current data can minimize inefficiencies and waste. When action is delayed or not forthcoming, you are simply monitoring performance and a continuous cycle of sub-par performance becomes the norm – undermining results, and employee commitment.

> Recently a front-line employee recounted their experience with a daily quality performance graph: "If scrap was to spike on a given day, this signals the need to solve the problem. We meet daily and review our quality metrics and take necessary action – often solving the problem. No longer do we have to wait until the Quality Team meets. We take action now – when data and memory are fresh. We avoid additional rework and product loss. We are proactive and proud."

The visual management of goals and measures allows Leadership to:

▶ Respond to the health of the CI initiative in real time.

▶ Coach teams or team members in new behaviors.

▶ Support the team members in meeting their goals.

Employees to:

▶ Focus daily on improvement.

▶ Reinforce new behaviors.

▶ Engage in their work in a meaningful way.

Figure 6: Team members discuss improvement results.

GOAL ALIGNMENT TAKEAWAYS

▶ Begin with a clear and compelling vision of the future, communicating to all WHY it is in the best interest of the organization, the employees, and stakeholders. Share the goals and strategy roadmap with steps, benchmarks, timelines, goals and KPIs.

▶ Create a visual workplace where the daily assessment of KPIs are made in each department and at each level of the organization. Everyone now becomes aware of how they are performing in pursuit of their goals.

▶ Make clear the expectations for colleagues in order to achieve the vision.

The OGSM and KPI Grid templates are available for download at www.thefivekeys.org

CASE STUDY: THE TWO SISTER SITES SOLVING THE PUZZLE

Goal Alignment: the process of aligning individual employee goals with the strategic goals of the organization, creating a direct line of sight which connects all members to a common purpose and plan.

Aligning goals and expectations throughout the organization is the point in time when we are able to take action on strategy and vision. Early into the CI journey for Site 1, we developed the understanding and discipline to articulate the vision and strategy and then cascade actionable goals to all teams throughout the site. The Leadership Team quickly realized how powerful this practice can be. Quarterly, goals are reassessed and tweaked for an optimal balance of improvement, relevance, and effectiveness. If strategy and objectives change during the year, goals are modified appropriately, enabling the business to pivot as necessary.

A good example occurred several years ago when new safety standards, equipment, and practices were introduced across the company worldwide. Changes were significant in this huge multi-year project. This safety initiative called for the installation of detection equipment, new processes, additional trainings, and a new set of behavioral safety requirements. Site 1 already maintained an excellent safety culture; however, the business mandate had now changed. By this time, many of the daily execution of "product out the door" goals had become unnecessary to visually manage. The new business requirements provided the opportunity to realign the organization around a very important endeavor.

A vision was created reflecting the importance of integrating the new safety initiative into the current culture. Objectives and milestones were defined, strategies developed and goals and measures cascaded throughout the site. The plan was communicated and expectations made clear.

The Steering Group responded by including aspects of the new safety program into the formal reward and recognition plan. Safety improvements were now to be expedited through the existing improvement idea process. In short order, Site 1 became the model site once again.

In contrast, Site 2 struggled to define yearly plant goals and objectives. This uncertainty made goals and expectations difficult to define in every department and front-line team - especially new behaviors associated with continuous improvement and safety. Employees understood the daily production goals and expectations well. The fear of failure made that clear.

Three years into our journey, I continued to experience a resistance to defining site metrics and cascading these to teams. They did just enough to "check the box." I was exhausted with the conversation, and had tried every approach possible of conveying the importance, short of doing it for them. In fact, I started to take heat from the corporate office about the effectiveness of the work I was doing with the site. On a third quarter visit, I made my daily tour of the facility, ending up in the leadership meeting office to check, once again, on the plantwide metrics. The visual management charts were not updated on the two metrics that had been chosen. I looked deeper to discover that a third metric was a sarcastic description of the current state. The metric was defined as "make it through the rest of the year without plantwide metrics" – the nine months of results were painted green for their success in this accomplishment!

I snapped a photo and sent it along with my last four quarterly site reports reiterating the same recommendations to the corporate office. The heat was no longer on me. A new level of accountability was added to the site. My fourth quarter and final visit of the year, was spent working with the leadership team defining and cascading goals, metrics, and expectations. The next year, the site made good progress!

ACCOUNTABILITY
IT STARTS WITH YOU

RESPONSIBILITY

MOTIVATION

BARRIERS

VISUAL MANAGEMENT

FOLLOW THROUGH

RECOGNITION

Accountabilty: an obligation or willingness to accept responsibility or to account for one's actions.

"You can assign tasks, but you can't force people to be accountable. Accountability is an act of will."

**—Robert (Bob) Reish,
Business Coach and Consultant**

Monday Morning

It happens, time and again, even in "world-class" organizations. You wrap up a planning meeting with 10 of your colleagues and create a list of items that need to be done. Mary will do this and John will take care of that. Everyone at your meeting is enthused and confident in the success of this improvement project. Each person confirms their support and willingness to help. Actions are mapped out and agreed, dates are set, everyone volunteered to help, so you are confident, you feel like you are good to go – off to a great start!

A month later, you meet again, and your worst fears become reality. Team members who said they would help did little, if anything, to move the project along. Colleagues look away avoiding your glance, heads are hung low. People are embarrassed and you feel angry and dismayed. So, what went wrong? Your colleagues are good people, they work hard, are very responsible; you think to yourself, "What in the world happened? I thought I could count on these folks — that they would follow through."

This scenario is one that you are likely to encounter as you lead change efforts. Despite the best of intentions, some colleagues will disappoint when it comes to follow-through.[38]

In this chapter we will consider:

▶ The Role of the CI Leader

▶ When and Why People Don't Follow Through

▶ Barriers

▶ Motivation

▶ Mistakes and Failures

▶ Visual Management

▶ Celebrating Success /Change Accelerator

---

38   Andrew Robertson, Nate Dvorak, Jennifer Robinson. Gallup. "Five Ways to Promote Accountability." https://www.gallup.com/workplace/257945/ways-create-company-culture-accountability.aspx2019.

CI Leaders

As the driver of your Continuous Improvement effort, a critical aspect of your success is your ability to enlist others in the effort and generate accountability. But despite the necessary reliance on others, it is the CI Leader who must create the environment where the drive for improvements is unrelenting. Without others' follow through, and a persuasive level of accountability, progress will not happen.

What You Can Do to Generate Greater Accountability and Follow-Through

As the leader of an improvement group, you expect those you are leading to perform in a certain predictable way. Your expectations are what you are attempting to hold your colleagues accountable for. These expectations are those things that you need others to do in order to move the CI initiative ahead.

Follow-through simply means that team members fulfill their assigned responsibilities and commitments. If team members fail to deliver on their commitments, you may be confronted with a litany of excuses, some legit and others not, offered by your teammates. These unfortunately do little to relieve you of your responsibilities to keep the project on track. Regardless of whether their excuses are genuine or merely alibis, the bigger problem is that they forestall needed actions. Worse yet, these delays demonstrate that the lack of accountability is acceptable.

While the temptation may exist to blame slow progress on the lack of follow-through by certain members of your team, it remains your obligation to keep the process on track and meet anticipated deadlines. That is why it is up to you to correct this problem.

Take Responsibility

The first step in tackling this universal challenge is for YOU to take responsibility for people's ability or failure to follow-through.

Ask yourself "What am I doing, or not doing, that is contributing to their non-compliance or lack of accountability?

By acknowledging that you have a role in your colleague's failure to deliver, it forces you to view the issue as one that you need to have a role in solving. *You have a team and you will solve it together.* It is also important to remind yourself that, at the end of the day, delays and failures will be laid at your feet, not those you lead. As happens so often in sports when a team underperforms, it is the coach who gets fired, not the players!

When People Don't Follow-through

The lack of follow-through can quickly derail even the most promising improvement efforts. In order to avoid this pitfall, understand the causes and plan accordingly.

First: consider the impact among your teammates. These occurrences, regardless of how rare, undermine your efforts. A colleague's failure to follow through affects team morale, their future involvement, and respect for you. If you fail to deal with this issue effectively, you will undoubtably keep dealing with this problem throughout the CI efforts.

Second: accept responsibility. As the CI Leader, you are ultimately responsible for the success or failure of the improvement initiative. You cannot allow the negative impact of unmet expectations to undermine your hard work and commitment to change.

Third: be proactive. An effective means of helping ensure colleagued follow through is by standardizing regular progress updates. With updates as a constant, you are able to monitor progress and eliminate surprises on due days. An additional tactic to bolster this approach is by incorporating "updates" as a feature in your visual management system.

Fourth: be unrelenting. <u>Most importantly</u>, you must confront unmet expectations —do not let it go!

Why People Don't Follow-through

In our experience, the reasons most cited by CI teams for the lack of follow-through include:

▶ Don't have the time.

▶ Don't have the resources.

▶ Lack of clarity (unsure what they were supposed to do).

▶ Lack of ability (they know what they are supposed to do, but do not have the skills).

▶ Low motivation.

▶ The task was too overwhelming.

▶ No repercussions if they don't succeed.

▶ They don't see the task as important.

▶ Laissez faire culture: In many organizations, the notion of accountability is just a wish.

This list can be divided into 2 main categories: Obstacles and Urgency.

Obstacles	Urgency
Lack of Clarity	The Status-Quo
Time Available	Competing Priorities
Skill/Ability	No repercussions
Resources	Resistance to Change

Regardless of the reasons, the challenge is to help your team be successful.

What If?

If you accept your colleague's rationale for not completing agreed upon tasks, what then?

There are only a few options for you to choose from:

▶ Accept that this person is unreliable, for whatever reason, and minimize your dependence on them to follow through.

▶ Reassign the work to someone else.

▶ Do the work yourself.

▶ Replace the person - if possible.

▶ Work with the colleague to avoid a repeat.

For some CI leaders, your position within your organization provides you with the authority to demand accountability or, at least, some measure of it.

Let's assume you are a mid-level person in your organization and recognize that threatening or issuing disciplinary actions are not in your arsenal. How then are you going to create the level of accountability necessary to accomplish your undertaking? First, focus on removing the obstacle. Second, increase team urgency.

Removing Obstacles

Lack of Clarity: This issue falls squarely to you to resolve. If people are unsure about your specific expectations, it becomes impossible to meet your requirements. To ensure clarity of assignments, we rely on the tried and true SMART formula to ensure that expectations are clear. For each assignment to fellow CI team members, follow the same SMART goal approach:

Specific	<ul><li>What specifically must be accomplished?</li><li>Why? What benefits will occur?</li><li>Provide details: Who, What, Why, When and Where?</li></ul>
Measurable	<ul><li>How will progress be measured? Metrics?</li><li>What are the milestones?</li><li>How will we know when we have succeeded?</li></ul>
Achievable	<ul><li>Are the goals, tasks and timelines realistic?</li><li>Do we have the talent, skills and commitment needed?</li><li>Are adequate time and other resources available?</li></ul>
Relevant	<ul><li>Does this goal align with our organization's vision?</li><li>Will achieving this goal move the organization forward?</li><li>Will others see the value in achieving this goal?</li></ul>
Time-Bound	<ul><li>What is the deadline for accomplishing this goal/task?</li><li>When will actions begin?</li><li>What negative impact is likely if unsuccessful in meeting the schedule?</li></ul>

Time: Time is often a very legitimate obstacle. For these circumstances, the agreed-upon deadline may need to be recalculated, the task broken down into smaller increments, and/or additional people added to the task.

Skill/Ability: Whether a team member has the skill or ability to follow through on an assignment is vital. We have found that people are very reluctant to admit that they do not possess the proficiency to complete an assigned task. When skill or ability is the real issue, other reasons are often cited as the reason the item was not completed. If the issue is skill-related, either assist by providing the training required to develop the skill, team them with someone who has the required skill, or assign that task to someone else.

Resources: If the lack of resources is cited for failure to meet a deadline, others on the team may be able to help provide or help secure the required resource. Sometimes, the request for additional resources is not feasible. Like all initiatives, there are budgets, other priorities and constraints that limit desired resources. Explore other options with your team and other leaders. If essential resources are absolutely necessary, personally make the request to those in a position to provide them.

Increasing Urgency

Change initiatives, by their very nature, upend many established work practices while introducing new behaviors to the workplace. In many instances, the changes necessary to the improvement effort are not necessarily welcomed. Yet, we hope that our colleagues, especially those working with us on implementation, will enthusiastically embrace and advocate for these changes.

In the real world, however, these hopes may go unfulfilled. You may find that some team members will be out-front driving the change, while others on the team may be hesitant to be seen beating the drum. The tentative members may be reacting to their own personal concerns or to those of their workmates. Regardless, the challenge is to increase motivation and rally colleagues to the cause. Your understanding of the four following motivation killers will contribute to building the support you require:

1. Challenge the Status-Quo

Complacency is major killer of change efforts. Absent a major crisis in your organization, most of your colleagues likely are content in the everyday execution of their present duties. They give a good day's work but are reluctant to sign up for more. Generally, most are unaware of changes occurring in your industry, what your competitors are doing, changing customer demands and future opportunities for your organization. While they may agree that improvements are needed, typically their days are full and additional commitments are not welcome. To gain traction here, the change effort needs to be viewed as *high-priority and a substantial benefit to both the organization and your colleagues.*

One approach to help demonstrate the significance of the effort is to request that a respected executive who has first-hand knowledge of the challenges ahead speak to them about the importance of the change initiative and meet with your team. Customer feedback also can strongly impact the perspectives of your colleagues. Even providing more information on your competitors, and their change efforts, can add insight and contribute to a sense of urgency.

2. Competing Priorities

Multiple priorities create a real-life tug-of-war for your CI teammates' work time and you must recognize that your initiative is just one of many demands competing for your colleague's attention. In order to focus a spotlight on your change initiative, your colleagues need to understand the overarching organizational strategy and why action on this effort is needed now. Continually restating and reinforcing the reasons for the change and the benefits to both the organization and the individual can be very helpful.

Communications, no matter how comprehensive, rarely exceed the need to know - so keep members up-to-date. Sharing progress and milestones achieved goes a long way to boost motivation. People want to be part of a win, and if this initiative looks like a winner, they will want to be on board.

3. No Repercussions

The old proverb "you can catch more flies with honey than with vinegar" still holds true. However, we also like this wise adage from Moliere: *"it is not only what we do, but also what we do not do, for which we are accountable."* As the CI champion, you have the right and the duty to call out colleagues who fail to deliver or follow through. Assuming that obstacles have been removed and it's only the lack of consequence that permits colleagues to disregard their commitments, then it's time to take the actions available to you.

4. Resistance to Change

Because resistance is so prevalent in any change effort, we suggest you re-read Dealing with Resistance – Normal and Predictable, Factors of Resistance and Make it Safe in the Leadership chapter.

Don't Run from Mistakes and Failures

Failure and setbacks are ingredients for a great story. Being accountable also means the sharing of bad news as well as the good. There will undoubtably be missteps to publicly share during your improvement efforts. Mistakes will be made.

While some setbacks may be impossible to plan for, acknowledging them when they occur, learning from them, and providing a course correction enhances your credibility and builds trust among your colleagues. Typically, when these failures do occur, others have already noticed. Taking responsibility allows you to quickly move on and demonstrates your adaptability and competence as a leader.

New Habits and Intentional Culture

Accountability is not just for project management. When shifting collective behaviors in an organization, keep in mind the principles and science of personal behavior change. In order to standardize and reinforce new routines, they must be daily, repeatable, measurable, and accountable. SOPs, Standard Work,

Visual Management and Reward and Recognition provide that necessary and consistent focus. Accountability to stabilize the natural regress of new behaviors is a must. *(See Standard Work and SOPs in Leadership Chapter)*

Visual Management of Commitments

Visually managing tasks and commitments is the most simple and effective means to reinforcing accountability. By creating a visual documentation of agreed-upon tasks, timelines, and responsible colleagues, you provide an up-to-date status of important aspects of your efforts for all to see. This transparency strengthens your communication strategy and stimulates greater interest and commitment to the effort. This process allows you to generate compliance without being heavy handed. The visual record speaks for itself. Our advice: keep it simple.

The power of visual management was driven home to us, many years ago, when visiting a manufacturing site in South Africa. Located on the left side of the entry hallway was an interesting display with over 100 wooden plaques, one for each company in their supplier chain. On each plaque was the name of the supplier company, the product or service they provided, and a smiling picture of that CEO. Directly across from this display, located on the opposite wall, were 5 similar plaques.

Finding this plaque arrangement curious, we inquired of the site manager about the configuration, with only 5 highlighted on one wall and a hundred on the other. Smiling, he replied, the wall with the hundred suppliers are companies that are great partners and doing a fine job. The wall, he explained, with only 5 were companies whose performance was unsatisfactory and soon to be replaced!

WOW! Talk about a visual to reinforce accountability!

The potency of visual management cannot be overstated. Visual management is simple and effective and when used correctly, it promotes transparency and accountability from the front line to the corporate office. While there are many different applications for visual management, each control should provide a quick status assessment and signal immediate action when necessary. The use of visual controls fosters accountability.

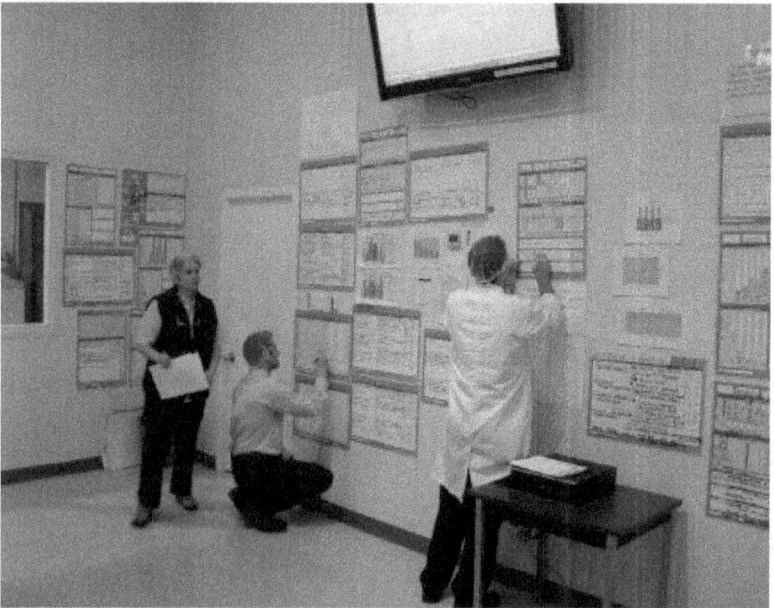

Figure 7: A frontline team updating their daily performance and action plans.

"Making accountability easier to see and execute is the objective that underlies lean management's way of thinking, its tools and approaches. But, do not confuse tools and techniques with the indispensable ingredient: you as chief accountability officer. Without you, no tools, no processes, no books can make lean implementation a healthy, growing, improving proposition." (Mann 2005)

– David Mann[39]

Variable Pay: Bonuses and Incentives

Variable or discretionary pay is a term that blankets commissions, bonuses, incentives and other compensation paid generally at the sole discretion of the employer. These pay programs are designed to reward certain behaviors and improved performance. In a 2018 survey by Payscale, nearly three-quarters of all organizations surveyed said that they offer some type of variable pay.[40] (Payscale .com 2018).

There are many types of bonuses (i.e., annual bonus, profit sharing, employee stock ownership plan ESOP, merit pay, retention bonus, stock options) and these are typically paid for goals that have been achieved. Often bonuses are part of employee's annual compensation package.

Incentive pay differs in that it is an award (paid in addition to base salary or wage) tied directly to future behaviors and performance. (i.e., piece-work, projects, improved performance, role specific,

---

39   David Mann. *Creating a Lean Culture*. (New York: Productivity Press, 2005).

40   Payscale.com. "Variable Pay Trends Into 2018: Who Gets It, What Types and Why." April, 2018.
     https://www.payscale.com/compensation-today/2018/04/variable-pay-trends#:~:text=While%20Individual%20performance%20is%20highly,team%20performance%20(40%20percent).

target based, job rotation, certifications, team/group, departments).

Tying Variable Pay to Continuous Improvement

If your organization currently utilizes variable pay programs, the opportunity to include specific continuous improvement behaviors and activities can be a program accelerator. Our experience is that when compensation is expressly tied to organizational objectives including continuous improvement and employee engagement, colleagues become more motivated and involved. Also consider team incentives as these are increasingly popular and based on the 2017 CBPR study, 38% of enterprise organizations utilize them.[41]

Beware: Unhealthy Competition

A word of caution — it is important to consider your current workplace culture, your workforce, and organizational history when designing variable pay programs. If the program is considered unfair or if individuals, teams, or departments are in unhealthy competition with each other, the results can be detrimental.

In your role as CI leader, advocating a constant focus on the common goals and objectives of the organization will help encourage colleagues to work together as a team not as individuals in the hunt for personal financial rewards.

Our Advice on Discretionary Pay

We believe and our experience confirms the old adage "what gets measured gets done" still holds true when it comes to employee

---

41   Payscale.com. "Variable Pay: Is There a Difference Between a Bonus and an Incentive?" June, 2017.
      http://www.payschle.com.compensation-today/2017/06/difference-bonus-incentive

compensation. By linking aspects of your continuous improvement initiatives such as improvements in performance, engagement, throughput, etc., with incentives and rewards elevates specific actions, behaviors, and results among managers and frontline colleagues.

Critical to discretionary pay success, however, is that pay practices must be fair, equitable, consistent, and understood.

Performance Reviews - Continuous Improvement Driver?

Annual performance reviews have been a part of the business scene here and across the globe for decades "By the 1940s, about 60% of U.S. companies were using appraisals to document workers' performance and allocate rewards. By the 1960s, it was closer to 90%.[42]

While annual performance reviews may have been well-intentioned, the actual practice of an employee sitting down with their manager, once a year, to assess their performance, possible promotion, wages, and goals for the coming year has become a nightmare for many front-line employees and managers alike.

"According to the Society for Human Resource Management, and as reported in *Slate*, "95% of employees are dissatisfied with their company's appraisal process. What's more, 90 percent don't believe the process provides accurate information."

---

42   Lydia Dishman. "The Complicated and Troubled History of the Annual Performance Review." *Fast Company*. November, 2018. https://www.fastcompany.com/90260641/the-complicated-and-troubled-history-of-the-annual-performance-review

Worse yet, an Adobe study found that performance reviews have no effect on how they do their job.[43]

As traumatic as an annual review can be for many rank-and-file employees, managers as well dislike the process. Managers hated doing reviews, as survey after survey made clear. Willis Towers Watson found that "45% did not see value in the systems they used." Deloitte reported that 58% of HR executives considered reviews an ineffective use of supervisors' time. In a study by the advisory service CEB, "the average manager reported spending about 210 hours—close to five weeks—doing appraisals each year."[44]

"There is no way to get better at something you only hear about once a year."

—Daniel Pink author of *Drive*

The End of Annual Performance Reviews?

As the evidence of a broken process continued to build over the decades, farsighted companies took the lead. "As you might expect, technology companies such as Adobe, Juniper Systems, Dell, Microsoft, and IBM have led the way. Yet they've been joined by a number of professional services firms (Deloitte, Accenture, PwC), early adopters in other industries (Gap, Lear, Oppenheimer Funds), and even General Electric, the longtime role model for traditional appraisals." By some accounts over one-third of U.S. companies already have replaced the annual review

---

43 Thomas Koulopoulos.. "Performance Reviews are Dead. Here's What You Should Do Instead." Inc. February, 2018. https://www.inc.com/thomas-koulopoulos/performance-reviews-are-dead-heres-what-you-should-do-instead.html

44 Peter Cappelli and Anna Tavis. "The Performance Management Revolution." October, 2016. https://hbr.org/2016/10/the-performance-management-revolution

with less-formal and more frequent conversations between managers and their employees.[45]

Coaching and Feedback - Better Options

From the perspective of a CI leader, we could find no evidence that annual coaching reviews generate greater employee accountability nor commitment to improvement initiatives and our decades of experience bears this out. We have found that providing employees frequent feedback and effective coaching is a far better way to establish and maintain accountability among your colleagues and build a culture of continuous improvement we all are striving for.

Recognition - Celebrating Successes

Recognition: honoring colleagues for performance or behaviors you would like to see repeated.

Throughout the span of your improvement efforts, there will be scores of occasions to recognize good work and progress – if you are looking for them. Identifying and seizing these opportunities should be very deliberate and not simply an ad hoc action that occurs occasionally.

A method we successfully deployed in organizations was establishing a monthly Continuous Improvement Meeting attended by department managers, team leaders and the site leader. In some organizations, frontline colleagues are also invited to these meetings, when possible. This meeting is facilitated by the CI leader with the express purpose of:

▶ Updating key site leaders on improvement efforts.

---

45   Ibid.

- ▶ Aligning managers in support of projects.

- ▶ Securing resources as needed.

- ▶ Sharing best practices.

- ▶ Fostering interest in improvement ideas.

- ▶ Healthy competition.

- ▶ Generating accountability and follow through.

- ▶ Providing recognition for work well done.

Sample Continuous Improvement Meeting Agenda

Item	Action	Person(s)	Time
1	Provides attendees the current status of improvement initiatives.	CI Leader	5 minutes
2	Each Department Manager reports on the progress within their areas of responsibility.	Area Managers	3 minutes each
3	Presentation of completed improvement initiatives and those under way in each team. Any requests for support from colleagues.	Team Leaders	3 minutes each
4	Report on Organization-wide performance, business priorities and challenges.	Site Leader	5 minutes
5	Recognition / Awards Presentation of the "Improvement of the Month" award to the Area Manager and Team Leader.	Site Leader	5 minutes

Whether you choose a CI meeting as outlined above or create your own method and structure, grasp the importance of a regularly scheduled get-together to share progress, provide recognition, and inspire others. As colleagues see and hear what is occurring across your site, they too will be inspired and motivated.

Seize the Moment

Everyone likes a pat on the back for a job well done, but far too often the recognition is too little and too late. It is almost a part of our culture to be humble and forgo praising ourselves and the work of others. We often hear that good performance is "what they get paid for." For CI leaders however, taking good performance for granted and waiting to celebrate positive steps in your change effort is a gross oversight.

Recognize that the implementation and sustainability of improvement efforts will not be defined by an occasional home run, but rather a succession of base hits. Celebrating these "base hits" and your colleague's good performance and milestones reached fosters greater commitment and builds confidence in the vision and strategy. We find another proven way to accomplish this is through a formal reward and recognition program

Formal Recognition Programs

A *formal recognition* program (a structured program with nominations, awards and public ceremony) is another proven approach known to stimulate employee interest. While such a method may or may not be new to your organization, it is a proven method to reinforce change efforts of all types.

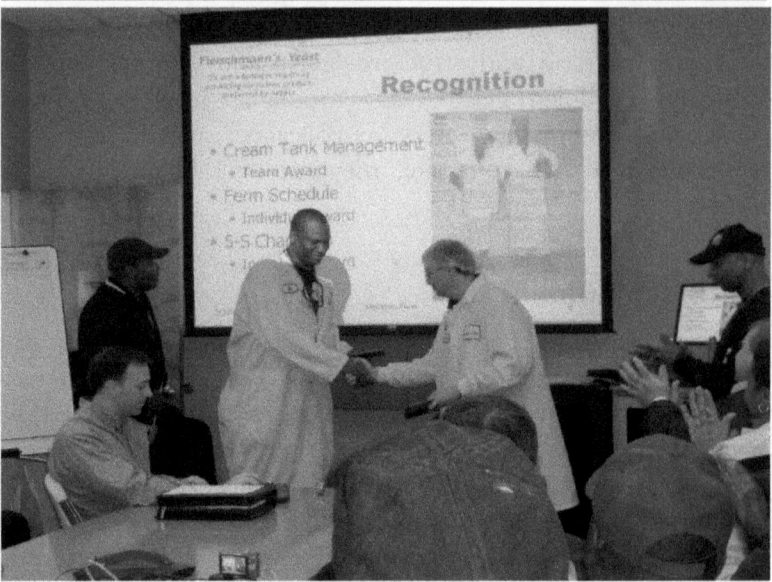

Figure 8: Recognition for a job well done.

By highlighting and recognizing key actions, behaviors, and habits, you tip your hat to those who are positively influencing others in the organization. In addition to recognizing individuals, whole teams and departments can share the spotlight as progress is made. A recognition program also provides an additional driver of accountability by acknowledging and supporting a culture of continuous improvement.

For example: if an organization is striving to develop a Visual Workplace 5S culture, the site can implement a monthly Recognition process that highlights key 5S behaviors such as Best Visual Management, 5S Sustainment of an Area, Highest 5S audit score, etc. These formal programs reinforce desired behaviors while identifying teams or individuals who may require additional support and coaching.

Risk and Reward

A discussion concerning "accountability" would be unfinished without consideration of "risk taking" by employees. Decades ago, the prevailing culture at the Ford Motor Company, like many other companies of that era, was one that if you took a risk and failed, your career ascent was over. You would not be fired, but your climb up the corporate ladder was finished. The culture adapted to this unwritten creed by managers and front-line employees alike, becoming risk-avoidant.

Employees at Ford learned that by keeping their heads down and avoiding risks they could look forward to steady employment, good pay, and retirement someday. What was sacrificed during these many years was innovation and steady improvement, vital attributes in the competitive auto industry. This environment and culture, spanning several decades, in many ways contributed to the decline at Ford.

Several attempts at cultural change were initiated by former Ford CEOs over the years, with limited success. It wasn't until Ford was near bankruptcy in 2006, and hired Alan Mulally as CEO, that this culture was forever turned on its head. Mulally came to Ford from The Boeing Company, where he was CEO and president of Boeing Commercial Airplanes. As a manufacturer of airplanes, Boeing was, in fact, a totally different industry with a totally different culture.

Within months after Mulally took the reins at Ford, he was forced to mortgage the entire company including factories, equipment, intellectual property, and even the famous Ford Blue Oval logo. The $23.6-billion line of credit he secured enabled Ford to finance new product development and avoid bankruptcy. Later, a concessionary labor agreement was negotiated with the United Auto Workers Union (UAW) intended to reduce production costs and how the union healthcare program was funded. The UAW supported Ford's restructuring and was a necessary partner in the effort. Mulally, and other Ford executives, also took symbolic salary cuts to communicate the difficulties the company faced.

As CEO, Mulally demanded new levels of openness and accountability; failures were no longer hidden and career-ending. Ford's top division leaders were now supported when taking risks. This new culture, combined with a rehabilitated business strategy and product line, was integral in bringing Ford back from the dead. This new level of accountability, without fear of punishment or reprisal, was a significant turning point in Ford Motor Company's recovery and continued their transformation as one of the world's leading automakers.[46]

Failures and Innovation

Ford is not alone in changing their stance on how they view accountability, risk taking, and failures. There are many examples of companies today that acknowledge and actually celebrate failed efforts, experimentation gone wrong, and ideas that simply did not work. The message to the workforce is that it is safe to try new things, to think innovatively, and to attempt to solve difficult

46   Bill Vlasic. "Choosing Its Own Path, Ford Stayed Independent." *New York Times*. April, 2009.
     https://www.nytimes.com/2009/04/09/business/09ford.html

problems. Creating a safe environment that recognizes and even rewards failed attempts at innovation build and support an intentional culture of creativity. Companies such as Google, 3M, Menlo Innovations WL Gore (Gore-Tex), Amazon, and Intuit are well-known for leading in this regard.

As much as accountability is essential, so too is honest recognition that progress often comes in fits and starts. There will be setbacks, mistakes will be made, experiments will fail and yet on somedays, good progress will be achieved.

How Recognition and Celebrating Successes Can Accelerate the Pace of Change

Introducing new behaviors and routines can be challenging to initiate and will take time to become the new standard. By providing colleagues with a clear set of expectations and procedures, gray areas are eliminated, common goals made clear, best practice becomes standardized, and together demonstrate and reinforce the commitment to continuous improvement. However, we all know that old habits die hard.

Given this ongoing challenge, we encourage you to make personal recognition and celebrating organizational successes part of your everyday thinking. The list below identifies several of the obvious benefits. In addition, as your colleagues step forward, they need to know that their commitment to the organization and willingness to change is truly appreciated. Your objective should be to:

1. **Validate New Behaviors:** Developing and reinforcing behaviors that are aligned with the improvement strategy is a critical outcome. These shifts in how we work may occur slowly, but should be recognized and applauded by the leadership. Although subtle, these new behaviors and habits will establish new norms that are the bedrock for a sustainable continuous improvement culture.

2. **Demonstrate Progress:** Achieving milestones and celebrating small incremental wins accelerates the pace of change. Even early supporters are looking for evidence that improvements are taking hold and the gains quantifiable. Sharing progress is vital to bringing the naysayers on board.

3. **Create Momentum:** As new behaviors and actions are recognized and celebrated, momentum begins to build. Employee involvement in this new initiative is no longer the exception, but is becoming the rule. For the "Late Majority," cited in the "Diffusion of Innovations" grid on page this additional evidence helps bring them onboard.

4. **Build Solidarity:** Celebrating the successes of both managers and rank and file colleagues reinforces the principle that we are in this effort together. For those cautiously awaiting additional evidence confirming support by others in the organization, they now have that proof.

Figure 9: Team Leader receives improvement trophy.

5. Reinforce The Vision: As recognition of milestones reached and good performance is celebrated, it confirms to the leadership and your organizations' key stakeholders, that the strategy is taking hold. Colleagues who may be "on the fence" become more inclined to visibly lend their support to the effort, as it no longer feels so "risky."

Make Recognition and Celebrating Successes Part of Your Everyday Routine:

In addition to a formal recognition program, daily affirmations make a huge difference.

▶ **Say "thank you."** Praise the good work of your colleagues. Let them know you recognize and appreciate their efforts.

▶ **Offer your appreciation regularly.** Don't wait for the perfect moment or the right audience to recognize good work. Make "well earned" praise a habit!

▶ **Write a note.** Not an email, but a handwritten "thank you" note. Short and sweet.

▶ **Communicate Successes Broadly.** Share your colleague's accomplishments with executives and rank and file colleagues. Feature good work in your newsletter and company-wide town hall meetings, etc.

▶ **Link recognition and successes to the Vision** you are all working toward.

Some Dos and Don'ts: Other Ways to Celebrate Successes and Provide Recognition.

DOs	DON'Ts
Be Timely: Don't wait too long. **Be Specific:** Give examples with details. **Be Sincere:** Don't blow smoke. Be honest. **Show Appreciation:** Thank them. Explain how it helps the effort. **Link to Vision:** Connect how their actions contributes to achieving the vision. **Encourage colleagues:** Provide feedback and share achievements. **Provide honest recognition:** As often as possible.	**Avoid:** Recognition that is ill-timed. Generalizations with no context or details. Disingenuous or false praise. Including everyone – this is special! Criticism. Rewarding actions not related to the Vision. Public recognition not appreciated by the recipient.

Non-monetary recognition:

▶ Devote a prominent column in your newsletter to CI.

▶ Have a top executive write a handwritten note to an outstanding performer or team.

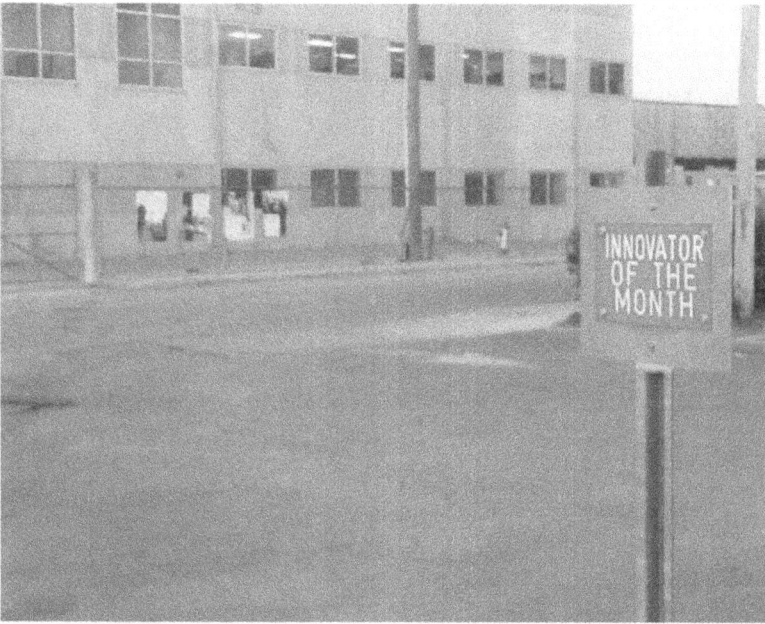

Figure 10: Parking privileges for this month's top innovator.

▶ Create a "Wall of Fame" recognizing significant achievements.

▶ Preferred parking.

▶ Rotate monthly a "trophy" for the outstanding team or department that best demonstrates the implementation of the improvement effort.

▶ Photo collection showing progress on the CI initiative.

▶ Before and after photos depicting progress.

▶ Choose an early adopter to represent their department in presenting progress to the Executive Leadership.

▶ A Managers Award for the best example of successful implementation.

▶ Make an update on the CI initiative a regular part of the leadership meetings / include participation by deserving colleagues for input and recognition.

▶ Allow colleagues to visit the work area where best practices are occurring.

▶ Invite a satisfied customer who is benefiting from your improvement efforts to visit and meet with colleagues.

Monetary recognition:

▶ Discretionary bonuses

▶ Profit Sharing

▶ Incentive pay

▶ Gain Sharing

▶ Paid time off

▶ Additional vacation

▶ Reward cards

▶ Gas cards

▶ Movie / Dinner certificates

▶ Sports tickets

* Advice: before initiating a monetary award program, broader implications should be carefully considered.

Look for opportunities to recognize and celebrate.

ACCOUNTABILITY TAKEAWAYS

▶ Require Accountability. If accountability is lacking, it is up to you to correct the problem - you must confront unmet expectations – you can't let it go. Accountability is essential to reinforce new habits and behaviors.

▶ Don't Run from mistakes and failures. There will undoubtably be setbacks and missteps. Taking responsibility allows you to quickly move on and demonstrates your courage, adaptability, and competence as a leader. Acknowledging setbacks signals to your colleagues that this is a safe environment and encourages them to take risks.

▶ Provide Recognition - Celebrating Successes. Seize the Moment. There will be scores of occasions to recognize the good work and progress made by your colleagues – if you are looking for them.

The SMART planning sheet is available for download at www.thefivekeys.org

🔍 CASE STUDY: THE TWO SISTER SITES SOLVING THE PUZZLE

Accountability: an obligation or willingness to accept responsibility or to account for one's actions.

Accountability coupled with behavior change is paramount to forging a new culture. By linking accountability to new behaviors gives the organization the opportunity to sustain and grow in a new direction.

The accountability precedent at Site 1 was established early on in the CI journey. From the onset, all seven senior leaders attended every coaching session with each departmental team. This level of engagement and commitment to their CI process demonstrated a level of accountability that would resonate throughout the organization. The message was clear, continuous improvement is part of our job.

It was decided at Plant 1 that they would merge aspects of their existing culture with new behaviors. New CI tools and duties would be integrated with the existing business systems. For example, the Maintenance Team was assigned work orders on a daily basis to predominantly address breakdowns and make repairs. In time, the system grew to include a higher percentage of preventative and predictive maintenance duties, 5S tasks, implementing improvements and conducting problem-solving sessions. Similar business systems were deployed for Operations, Administration, Logistics, Laboratory etc.

Employees were accustomed to relying on these systems to guide their daily work. Team meetings, 5S duties, autonomous maintenance tasks, additional quality inspections and other improvement assignments could be included in colleague's daily duties. This seamless integration with established business processes generated the understanding that continuous improvement was part of the daily business, daily tasks and as accountable and important as any other aspect of their day.

Adding further importance and accountability to following through on these new assignments, managers conducted daily "walk-throughs" and observations. In doing so, managers bolstered accountability and reinforced collective plantwide daily CI behaviors. The Site 1 Plant Manager continually stressed: "if you don't follow through on the small tasks and daily discipline, how would you expect my team to dig into the hard stuff?"

Site 1 further displays their commitment to accountability through the visual management of long-term improvement projects. Plans are developed with roles, actions and deadlines and posted prominently on the board. Every Wednesday, at the manager meeting, a progress review takes place and the board is updated. This regimen has instilled a new habit and provides a safe environment to offer support and ensure projects stay on schedule.

Finally, an additional level of accountability and support is added during each of my quarterly visits. My visit typically opens with a meeting with all managers and key members of the CI Steering Group. At this time, we review open action items and progress since my last visit. New actions are visually captured, supported and action plans made.

In contrast, Site 2 developed a unique method of keeping visual management under wraps and thereby avoiding accountability. From early on, each team did meet just about every-day to review performance and solve problems. Visual management was only available for the meeting and then tucked away under a staircase or unused hallway. The rationale given was that there was not enough wall space or areas to accommodate the visual management during the workday. It took time to convince the site that openly displaying visual management supports new behaviors and builds accountability - not only for frontline teams, but for management as well.

This resistance to visual management contributed to a lack of accountability and played-out in many ways. Long-term projects were slow to take shape. Daily issues were forgotten as new ones surfaced. Standard Operating Procedures (SOPs) were inconsistent and varied throughout the site. Daily checklists and cleaning obligations varied from shift to shift. And unfortunately, safety issues got the best of them due to the lack of accountability; the need to follow procedures, secondary checks and standard training. This was the culture – a lack of accountability. The necessary shift in culture and sustainment of new behaviors was dependent on Leadership embracing accountability, shaping it into a metric, cascading expectations, visually managing, and walking the walk.

Resources: Return on Investment

Business Resources: human, financial, materials and knowledge factors that can be drawn on by a person or organization in order to function effectively. Anything and everything that helps a company operate.

Return on Investment (ROI): the amount of return on a particular investment, relative to the investment's cost.

"Business purpose and business mission are so rarely given adequate thought is perhaps the most important cause of business frustration and failure."

— Peter Drucker

Resources & ROI (Return On Investment)

A major challenge to creating a sustainable continuous improvement culture is securing adequate resources and commitment – *especially over the long haul*. Every organization must continually justify their improvement initiatives and justification is generally measured as Return on Investment (ROI) – in other words, money.

The return on the investment from improvement initiatives encompasses far more than just hard financial benefits alone. This chapter is intended to provide you with additional measures, other than just financial, that will demonstrate to your colleagues and especially the executive leadership that their ongoing commitment to Continuous Improvement is worth the cost and effort.

As the CI champion, you are in competition with other initiatives for your organization's commitment and resources. Whether it be measured in money, time, or talent, making the case for adequate and ongoing support will often fall to you. Your voice is critical in building the understanding that the benefits of CI extend far beyond each quarter's earnings and represent the long-term future of the organization.

To assist you in securing needed resources, we cover in this chapter:

▶ Myths and CI Efforts

▶ Overcoming Obstacles

▶ Measures and Creating Value

▶ The "Balanced Scorecard"

▶ Creating a Balanced Scorecard for Continuous Improvement

▶ Challenges on the Frontlines

▶ Key Resources

Dealing With the Facts

For nearly four decades, there has been the perception that CI efforts fail to deliver promised results. A 1979 study is often cited to suggest that 70% of change efforts fail. This misquoted and twisted fable forms a backdrop for heightened scrutiny of improvement expenditures and demands for a corresponding return on investment. The article below explains how this folklore originated and what has occurred since:

The insidious myth that change initiatives usually fail is disturbingly widespread. Many experts, for example, state that 70% of change efforts fail, but a 2011 study in the Journal of Change Management, led by the University of Brighton researcher Mark Hughes found that there is no empirical evidence to support this statistic. In fact, there is no credible evidence at all to support the notion that even half of organizational change efforts fail.

Hughes traces the mythical 70% failure rate back to the 1993 book Reengineering the Corporation, in which authors Michael Hammer and James Champy stated: "our unscientific estimate is that as many as 50 percent to 70 percent of the organizations that undertake a reengineering effort do not achieve the dramatic results they intended."[47]

From that point on, Hammer and Champy's "unscientific estimate" took on a life of its own. A 1994 article in the peer-review journal Information Systems Management presents Hammer and Champy's estimate as a fact and changes "50 percent to 70 percent" to just "70 percent."

In Hammer's 1995 book, The Reengineering Revolution, *he attempts to set the record straight:*

"In Reengineering the Corporation, *we estimated that between 50 and 70 percent of reengineering efforts were not successful in achieving the desired breakthrough performance. Unfortunately, this simple*

---

47   Nick Tasler, "Stop Using the Excuse 'Organizational Change is Hard,'", *Harvard Business Review* (July 19, 2017).

descriptive observation has been widely misrepresented and transmogrified and distorted into a normative statement...There is no inherent success or failure rate for reengineering.[48]

Despite Michael Hammer's clarification, the 70 percent statistic has continued to be cited as fact, including in *Harvard Business Review* articles and books.

Granted, there is some ambiguity surrounding the success of change initiatives. For example, when consultants at McKinsey surveyed 1,546 executives in 2009, 38percent of respondents said "the transformation was completely or mostly successful at improving performance, compared with 30 percent similarly satisfied that it improved their organization's health."[49]

Based on the numbers from the McKinsey study, it would be tempting to conclude that since only 30-38percent of change initiatives are "completely/mostly successful," then 62-70 percent must be failures. However, the McKinsey authors added that "around a third [of executives] declare that their organizations were 'somewhat' successful on both counts."

In other words, a third of executives believed that their change initiatives were total successes, and another third believed that their change initiatives were more successful than unsuccessful. But only "about one in ten admit to having been involved in a transformation that was 'completely' or 'mostly' unsuccessful."

Therefore, pointing to the McKinsey study as evidence for "a 70 percent failure rate is like saying that every time a baseball player steps up to the plate and doesn't hit a home run, that player has

48   James A. Chanpy and Michael M. Hammer. *Reengineering the Corporation.* (New York: Harper-Collins. 1993)

49   Jack Martin Leith. "70% of Organizational Change Initiatives Fail" Fact or Fiction? 2019. http://jackmartinleith.com/70-percent-change-failure-rate/

failed. But that isn't true in baseball any more than it is true in organizations." The McKinsey results show that around 60 percent of change initiatives are somewhere between a base-hit and a home run, and only 1 in 10 are complete strikeouts.[50]

Obstacles To Overcome

Besides the negative myth described above, there are the ghosts of past improvement attempts in organizations, whether successful or not. The "flavor of the month" chant will surface whenever employees hear of a new change initiative. This labeling conveniently offers cover for colleagues to trivialize the effort and provides them with justification for withholding their support – *including resources.*

Add to the mix the actual fallout from past improvement efforts, now neglected or abandoned. While real monetary outlays — for wages, consultants, materials, software, travel, etc. — may have been sizeable, these costs may pale in comparison with the negative long-term impact of past incomplete efforts on employees. Intangible factors such as the loss of trust in leadership, increased cynicism, resistance to future change efforts, and negative personal impact can be more disheartening than the financial losses.

Whether the history of improvement efforts in your organization is negative or positive, continual improvement remains an imperative. Accept that some resistance and skepticism will likely be present in both the leadership ranks as well as among rank-and-file front-line colleagues – it's a fact of life. Regardless, in your role as CI leader, a way forward must be charted and presented in

---

50   Nick Tasler. "Stop Using the Excuse 'Organiational Change is Hard'." July, 2017. https://hbr.org/2017/07/stop-using-the-excuse-organizational-change-is-hard

such a way that attracts both change advocates and the naysayers to the cause – and you can do it!

> **Message to the organization's top leaders:** Make clear your commitment to the improvement initiative and ensure that your commitment for adequate resources is forcefully communicated to the front-line managers and employees. Knowing you have their backs, both in commitment to the endeavor and providing the resources it will require, are critical elements in the success of your efforts

Identify Broader Measures

Michael J. Mauboussin in a *Harvard Business Review*[51] confirms the importance of using broader metrics to evaluate.

> *"The metrics companies use most often to measure, manage, and communicate results—often called key performance indicators—include financial measures such as sales growth and earnings per share (EPS) growth in addition to nonfinancial measures such as loyalty and product quality."* He goes on to say: ... *"these have only a loose connection to the objective of creating value. Most executives continue to lean heavily on poorly chosen statistics, the equivalent of using batting averages to predict runs."*

The relevance of purely financial measures is obviously limited, but their importance is distorted because executives and most managers are themselves measured by whether they meet financial targets. Without question, profits are necessary for survival in a for-profit organization. That said, a successful and vibrant

---

51   Michael J. Mauboussin. "The True Measures of Success." *Harvard Business Review.* October, 2012. https://hbr.org/2012/10/the-true-measures-of-success

enterprise is more than its bottom line and it is necessary to identify those other measures of its progress and value.

Creating Value

Launching a continuous improvement initiative provides an opportunity to introduce several important actions and related measures that bring value and long-term health and growth to the organization. These may include:

▶ implemented process improvements.

▶ successful problem solving.

▶ higher employee engagement.

▶ improved customer service and satisfaction.

▶ number of employees trained.

▶ level of employee satisfaction.

▶ employee retention.

▶ others.

The real strategic benefit lies in creating a sustainable culture that develops new capabilities among your colleagues to identify and implement process improvements, solve problems, and better deliver goods and services to your customers. CI is the vehicle that will drive improvements across all aspects of the entire business, and as such, cannot and should not be assessed by financial benefits alone.

It's Hard to See the Forest for the Trees - Justifying a CI Initiative

Several years ago, we were introduced to an organization by their corporate office. We began exploring work with the large machine shop that provides parts for the high-tech aerospace industry. As discussions began, the site had numerous questions regarding introducing a CI program - concerns ran the gamut:

- **Adding front-line team meetings**: "operators should be operating when on the clock; we don't need more meetings!"

- **Cost of launching a formal CI program**: "how do we justify these costs; what's the payoff?"

- **Bringing in consultants**: "we have an internal CI department that we already pay – we don't need any help."

After some time, we were able to gain trust within the organization and helped them assess the huge cost of holding inventory, the financial penalties associated with late projects, and overtime payments needed to correct errors and expedite orders at the end of each month. Doing some quick math, it became apparent that the company spent much more maintaining their current inefficiencies than it would cost to introduce a CI program. It was at this point that the project cautiously moved forward.

We worked with the CI team and suggested certain process changes and the introduction of a team-based work system. Before long, the organization became convinced that these improvement efforts were the best way forward and a prudent path out of the current state of high inventory, missed deadlines, increasing rework and scrap, and expedited orders.

Within six months, major improvements across the site were under way. The 10-minute daily team meetings paid off big time! Machine operators had measured and identified ways to reduce the amount of scrap materials produced in one small area of the plant. They were astounded at the monthly recurring cost of $40,000 in scrap material alone. This loss of product also led to a domino effect of high inventory, rework, late deliveries, higher shipping fees, longer lead times, and additional overtime. The team had found a way to error-proof their operation and then train and communicate these preventative action steps to the rest of the site. From that day forward, operations reduced its scrap to less than $100/month.

The perpetual cost savings of $40,000/month has paid for the initial CI investment more than 1,000-fold at this time of writing. In fact, one month's overall savings more than covered the initial investment that the site was so apprehensive about and halted the domino effect of exponential hidden costs to the company.

Furthermore, this dynamic problem-solving culture continues to respond to daily challenges while providing an environment of high engagement and employee satisfaction.

The 'Balanced Scorecard'

Over the years we have found that the "Balanced Scorecard" approach, created by Robert Kaplan and David Norton of Harvard Business School in the 1990s,[52] *is especially well-suited to support and guide continuous improvement initiatives.* The work of Kaplan and Norton was driven by the popular tendency by businesses to focus, almost entirely, on financial measures. This "lagging indicator" became a poor guide to preparing businesses for the future as these financial measures only reflected what had occurred in the past – how you performed last month, last quarter, last year. What was missing were "leading" measures or indicators as to how an organization was likely to fare in the future. These measures were now seen as vital information to executives in order to enable their organizations to prepare strategically for their future.

Through their work, Kaplan and Norton created a management system, still dominant in business planning today, dubbed "Balanced Scorecard." Their creation expanded management's focus from annual short-term profits to include identifying, developing and implementing strategies, goals, and measures to ensure long-term success. They introduced four different business aspects to form a comprehensive planning and measurement approach. These differing perspectives, through which the business is viewed and success measured, are: Financial, Customer, Business Processes and Learning and Growth.

---

52   David P. Norton & Robert S. Kaplan. *The Balanced Scorecard.* (Cambridge: Harvard Business Press. 1996.)

The Balanced Scorecard

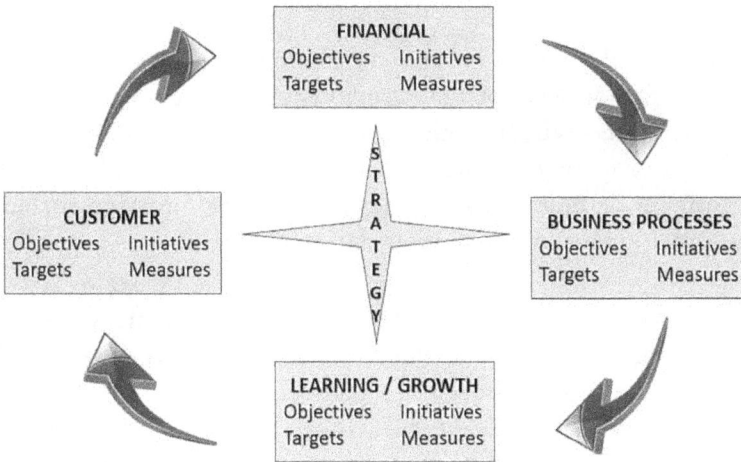

Financial Perspective: The financial well-being of your organization is the ultimate "bottom line." Is the strategy promoted by your executive team delivering the anticipated financial results? Are shareholders satisfied? Measures typically include: earnings before interest and taxes (EBIT), net cash flow, gross profit margin, liquidity ratio, economic value added (EVA).

Business Perspective: The internal business perspective assesses how smoothly your business is running. Quality, Throughput and Cost-effectiveness are the focus. Improvement efforts are continual and closely monitored.

Learning and Growth Perspective: The learning and growth perspective looks at the overall culture of the organization. Are people knowledgeable of the strategy, goals, and objectives laid out by the leadership team? Do employees collaborate and share knowledge? Are you staying ahead of your competition? What are the latest industry trends? Is training offered, are people learning new skills and competencies? Are continuing education and promotional opportunities available? Is technology in your organization up to date? Are your colleagues equipped and trained? Often, measures include employee satisfaction, retention, and training.

Customer Perspective: The customer perspective focuses on the satisfaction level of the people who buy your products and services. Are your customers pleased? Is your customer base growing or getting smaller? What are the new demands of your customers or potential customers? Customer measures include customer satisfaction, retention, and market share.

These four perspectives are not simply independent measures, but are all connected in determining the future prospects and financial health of an organization. For example: investments in learning and growth lead to greater employee involvement which contributes to problem-solving and process improvement which leads to improved customer satisfaction and growth and ultimately generates greater financial performance.

In developing a balanced scorecard each perspective should include Objectives, Measures, Targets, and Initiatives. The following table shows how these perspectives can be organized.

	Objectives	Measures	Targets	Initiatives
Financial				
Business Process				
Learning and Growth				
Customer				

Objectives: major direction such as "improve manufacturing efficiency."

Measures: a standard unit used to express the size, amount, or degree.

Targets: specific desired outcomes that support achievement of the objectives.

Initiatives: projects or programs undertaken, in the near-term, to reach targets and achieve specific objectives.

How a Balanced Scorecard Can Support and Protect Your CI Efforts

Generally, Continuous Improvement is thought of as a stand-alone, single-focus strategy. When viewed from this perspective, the value of CI is restricted only to improving internal business processes (planning, production, and service) and limits the arena in which CI leaders can demonstrate their worth.

While the Balanced Scorecard was originally developed as a performance measurement system, the broadened CI perspective allows for:

▶ Clarifying and Communicating Strategy: Articulating specific actions and the benefits of CI across a broader range of business perspectives, shifts the emphasis from short-term process improvements, to the long-term success of the entire enterprise.

▶ Planning, Setting Targets and Initiatives: Challenging and realistic improvement targets are determined and pursued for each of the four perspectives and corresponding initiatives.

▶ Feedback, Learning and Tweaks: Accurate feedback on initiatives and outcomes provides the organization with valuable learning and the opportunity to celebrate, modify, change, discard or replace an initiative, based on real data and experience.

Creating Your CI Balanced Scorecard

Whether you have begun your CI effort or are considering launching an initiative, building agreement among the executive leadership and your colleagues on desired outcomes and success criteria will support your effort long into the future. Creating and adopting a "balanced scorecard" will untether you from the focus on short-term cyclical financial results. By design, the balanced scorecard provides a comprehensive long-term assessment of the benefits of your improvement efforts.

The objective of every CI initiative is to contribute to achieving the organizations' strategy. As you develop your scorecard, we offer the following advice: **Always link Continuous Improvement Goals and Measures to the Corporate Strategy.**

For example: Upon completing their strategic planning, the fictitious Brownfield Cosmetic Company's executive leadership team created this vision for their future: *"To be the most competitive and reliable manufacturing site in the Brownfield Group."* The executive leadership identified four strategic goals that were critical to achieving this vision:

▶ **Increase throughput through teamwork and personal accountability.**

▶ **Reduce rework and defects.**

▶ **Expand customer loyalty.**

▶ **Revitalize our product portfolio.**

With these four strategies identified, each CI effort should contribute to at least one of these strategic objectives. Without a clear connection to these high-level corporate imperatives, your CI effort will be viewed as just another one of many interesting, but low-priority programs. When competing for resources, articulating and proving value is essential; "interesting" concepts won't succeed.

Using the Brownfield Group example, there are numerous CI initiatives that contribute directly to the 4 corporate strategic goals and clearly are beneficial to the short-term and long-term viability of the organization.

	Objectives	Measures	Targets	CI Initiatives
Financial	Increase throughput through teamwork and personal accountability.	Number of problems identified and solved that contributed to schedule attainment.	2 problems resolved per week.	Weekly assessment of schedule attainment failures and appropriate remedial actions.
Business Process	Reduce rework and defects.	Assess financial costs of rework and defects.	Reduce the cost of rework and defects by 50% in 12 months.	Engage team in identifying causes and conduct weekly problem-solving sessions.
Learning and Growth	Revitalize our product portfolio.	New product possibilities.	Identify 1 new viable product possibility each quarter.	Collect and analyze data on current product usage and identify customer trends.
Customer	Expand customer loyalty.	Customer complaint response time.	Respond to each customer complaint in 48 hours or less.	Assess daily products related to complaints, identifying and implementing feasible corrective measures within 30 days.

By focusing not on just one perspective (Financial), but all four perspectives in the Balanced Scorecard (Financial, Business Process, Financial, Learning and Growth, and Customer), we deploy our skills and tools to be applied to a variety of differing challenges and areas of the business. In doing so, CI leaders can demonstrate value as an arsenal capable of improving the organization and assisting colleagues in every worthwhile and vital aspect of the business.

Frontline Challenges

While the Balanced Scorecard approach can play a huge role in securing resource commitments at the top leadership levels, securing necessary resources on a daily basis to sustain your efforts at the front lines presents different challenges. Time, talent, and money are likely to always be a scarce resource on the front lines and securing what your CI initiative demands is likely to require a shift from business as usual.

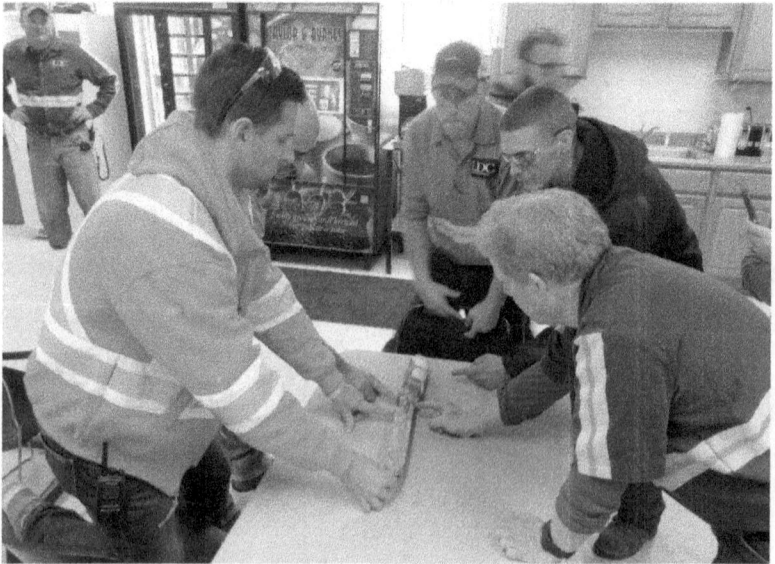

Figure 11: Colleagues work together to identify process improvements.

At the outset, organizations dedicated to continuous improvement must recognize that it is necessary to distribute resources differently. *This redistribution must be done in a way that maintains the current requirements for quality, safety, throughput, cost efficiencies, etc., while also supporting new efforts and behaviors.*

The investment in CI should be considered prior to implementation. As the CI Leader, you will need to define these specific needs and justify expenditures. Depending on the scope of the improvement initiative, your requests will likely be evaluated on anticipated cost savings and performance improvements. By allocating adequate resources to the CI project, your organization demonstrates its commitment, which will secure a shift in collective behaviors.

Resources Needed to Support New Behaviors

As a CI representative, it will be important to be aware of the necessary redistribution of your finite resources available to you. How you negotiate reutilization may determine how well new behaviors grow and sustain your program. For example, you may provide a formal problem-solving process training to your colleagues. But, without allowing ample time and the appropriate talent during the workday to actually address problems, it will unlikely be utilized nor become a new habit and process. The resources, *time and people*, must be available for problem solving and implementing fixes. Without them, each occurrence takes on a life of its own ceding to pressure to move on to the normal day-to-day tasks. To shift the culture from ad-hoc problem solving to a standardized approach requires a shift in thinking, behaviors, and appropriate resources.

The Cart in Front of the Horse

A challenge often encountered when launching front-line teams is the allocation of designated times for these groups to meet. The concept is that each day, front-line colleagues participate in a short 5-10-minute team meeting to discuss their work plan, manage goals, identify problems, and generate improvement ideas. The idea of stopping production, even for a few minutes, may seem counterintuitive to managers responsible for daily production quotas. However, if time away from production is only viewed as "lost throughput," then opportunities to improve quality, cost-effectiveness, safety, and even increasing throughput will never benefit from the wisdom and experience of the people doing the work. Now that is counterintuitive!

Those organizations which embark on a CI initiative may wrestle with the conflict of Direct Labor Resources vs CI Process Resources. Realistic planning and front-end investments are, most often, a prerequisite to a solid commitment and launch.

Key Resources Generally Required

Time

All sustainable CI initiatives require an investment in time. Regardless of the improvement focus (i.e., Kaizen projects, 5S implementation, Value-stream Mapping, Problem Solving, etc.), in order to be effective, management must designate time to conduct these activities. It is important to establish a defined and standard process for holding meetings, problem solving, and assessing improvement ideas. Standardizing these activities saves time in the long run, reinforces behaviors, and bolsters the commitment and engagement throughout the organization.

Key areas of time utilization for CI:

▶ **Meetings** – effective meetings drive results.

▶ **Improvements** -providing time to staff to implement improvements.

▶ **Reward and Recognition** – taking the time to recognize employees.

▶ **Problem Solving** – incorporate "PS" into the work schedule.

▶ **Kaizen/Improvement Projects, 5S**

Money

Every organization that is committed to launching and sustaining a successful CI program must be prepared to make the ongoing financial investments necessary to support this new direction. In addition to the direct costs for labor, training, and materials, some initiatives also require associated financial requirements.

Things to consider:

Improvements brought forward by employees –Regardless of the improvement tools your organization chooses, you should expect an avalanche of recommendations and possible solutions to problems experienced by colleagues who do the work on a daily basis. Their improvement recommendations often provide savings that immediately offset the initial program costs. Be prepared to invest in these suggestions – if new ideas stall, team members interest will diminish.

Invest in Experts – Wisely chosen experts and consultants can bring experience and a skill set to CI process improvement that can save an organization time and money by avoiding pitfalls. Outside experts can suggest Best Practice based on their experience with other organizations, build internal capacity, and provide an honest, external analysis on the initiative's progress.

Technology – Technology can play an important role in your improvement initiatives. Examples of technology positively impacting communications, productivity, inventory management, customer service, marketing, financial services and learning are noteworthy. If the introduction of new technology is planned, provide up-front training plans and cite what changes are expected and the positive impact for the organization and its members. Allay fears by sharing what assistance will be provided.

Reward and Recognition – A robust "R&R" program is always recommended to reinforce good performance and foster engagement. A list of reward and recognition options can be found in the Accountability Chapter.

Training

Besides the orientation employees receive when joining an organization and the occasional on-site safety training initiatives, job training often tends to be compartmentalized and provided to the specific skill set or classifications in which colleagues perform their day-to-day work. Regulatory requirements and job specific tasks often limit the remaining time an organization may allocate for any additional training needs.

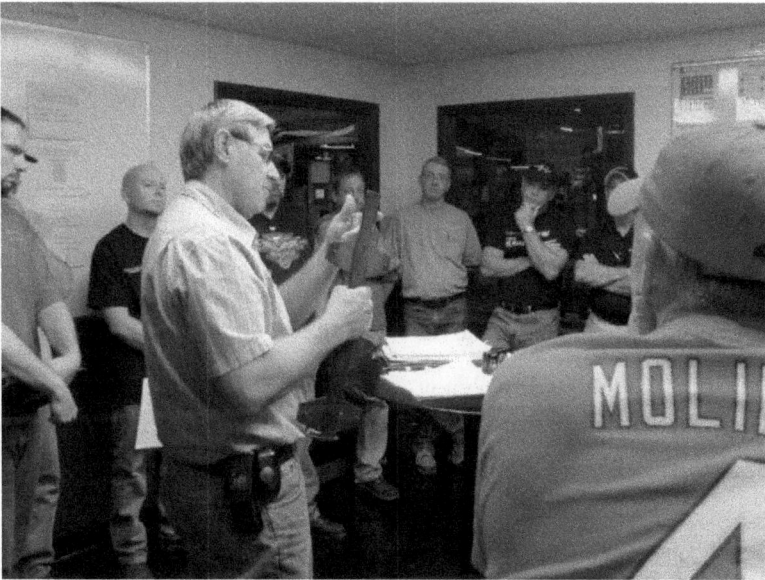

Figure 12: Team takes time to meet in order to tackle production problem.

"It is not enough to do your best; you must know what to do, and then do your best."

— **Deming**

The lack of ongoing training and skill building is often a missed opportunity for improving performance results and increasing employee retention. CI initiatives can spotlight training opportunities beneficial to both the organization and its members. Providing additional development for employees is a two-fer: both the organization and members benefit.

> A three-year research project commissioned by Middlesex University's Institute for Work Based Learning among an average 4,300 workers per annum revealed that a huge percentage (74%) felt they were not achieving their full potential at work and, as a result, would value access to more development opportunities.

RESOURCES
TAKEAWAYS

▶ As a leader of a continuous improvement initiative, you will likely be called upon to justify and demonstrate an appropriate return on investment. Identify the key resources needed to support the CI Initiative.

▶ Establishing a long view with comprehensive measures for assessing the impact of improvement initiatives is a vital step in assuring adequate resource allocation and sustainability. A reallocation of resources supports culture change.

▶ Utilizing a "Balanced Scorecard" for assessing the CI effort can demonstrate positive impact across a wide array of relevant measures. Results focused solely on savings are a lagging indicator and falsely reflect the benefits to the organization.

▶ Supporting CI initiatives at the front line with the appropriate resources (Time, Money, Training) takes planning. This redistribution must be done in a way that maintains the current requirements for quality, safety, throughput, cost efficiencies, etc., while also supporting new efforts and behaviors.

The Balanced Scorecard template is available for download at www.thefivekeys.org

🔍 CASE STUDY: THE TWO SISTER SITES SOLVING THE PUZZLE

Resources: human, financial, materials and knowledge factors that can be drawn on by a person or organization in order to function effectively. Anything and everything that helps a company operate.

Every organization, committed to CI, must decide how much of their limited resources they are willing to obligate to support their CI culture. To arrive at this answer, Site 1 follows this process: Each new year starts with an assessment of priorities that will impact the business. This is based upon a Balanced Scorecard assessment. Because continuous improvement has become the norm, "the way we do business," the site determines the level of CI support required for each priority. Time, money, training, and non-direct labor activities are considered to determine how resources can be appropriately distributed across the organization. As the year progresses, periodic reassessments and redistributions take place as necessary. At Site 2, resources required for CI initiatives are determined as required on an ad-hoc basis. Over time, both sites agreed that the yearly investment is aptly justified by improved annual business results.

The comparison between the two sister sites and their utilization of resources is notable. Site 1 never hesitated to make available the necessary staff, team members, and any training required for any CI activities. Our time together was always considered valuable. Prior to each of my two-day quarterly visits, site-management and I would develop a detailed agenda planning out each hour of each day. No time was wasted. Our planning was always done, well in advance, to assure the availability of personnel and materials required.

At Site 2 the experience was very different. On early visits, developing an agenda was *always* a challenge. For example, prior to a scheduled quarterly visit, I attempted to secure an agenda with time allocated for training sessions with both management and front-line teams. Despite emails and phone calls placed by me to the site manager, repeated over a period of several weeks, I could not secure a commitment. Finally, just days prior to my visit, I received an e-mail indicating that an agenda, as requested, would be prepared and available for me at 8 a.m. on our first meeting day. When I arrived that morning, there was no agenda and no employees with whom to meet - no planning had taken place. As a result, the first day of my two-day visit was spent attempting to cobble together an agenda and secure meeting times with managers and front-line team members. A wasted training day – resources squandered.

This inaction or passive resistance by management at Site 2 was, unfortunately, not an isolated incident. On a separate occasion, upon arriving for my quarterly visit, the plant experienced a process failure. Not surprisingly, this required "all hands on deck" as production was halted. Fortunately, after several hours, the issue was finally remedied and operations resumed. This was clearly a teachable moment: to assist the team in identifying the possible causes for the failure, and later, conduct an in-depth problem-solving session to explore preventative measures.

The following morning, I attended the team meeting eager to offer my assistance. The meeting was poorly attended as team members were focused on starting their daily routines. Some members were clearly not interested, turning their backs to the team meeting. The issues of the previous day were mentioned by the supervisor, but only in the context of how important it was to play catch up today. I learned that this process failure was not unusual, had happened in the past, and was likely to recur.

The singular focus on immediately recouping lost production took precedent over the benefits of capturing relative data concerning the mishap, while still fresh among team members. An investment in time and talent to meet and focus on permanently solving problems was not, as yet, part of the culture.

My final example highlights the importance of the link between providing adequate resources for the growth and development of CI culture. Site 1 made the investment early on to clearly define systems to support the new CI initiative. The Reward and Recognition program was one particular investment that paid off. As new skills, tools, and processes are integrated into the business, the Reward and Recognition program is ready to incorporate these items. Each month offers an opportunity for the Steering Group to identify and challenge teams in one or two areas of growth.

Held each month, the meeting includes lunch followed by one hour dedicated to: site performance, updates, new initiatives, and awards given. The R&R meeting supports the other four keys and strengthens culture:

▶ Leadership has the opportunity to "Walk the Walk," recognize good performance and support team members.

▶ Increases in employee engagement by rewarding individuals and teams who achieve results by working together.

▶ Goal Alignment is reinforced as links between daily tasks and new behaviors are associated with bottom-line results.

▶ The "friendly competition" for recognition between teams, adds an additional level of peer accountability.

The dedication of resources (time, talent and money) to the CI effort often becomes a leading indicator of how successful your initiative is likely to be.

SECTION 3

FIXES

Every Continuous Improvement leader has experienced setbacks and failure; this is a normal part of learning and the old adage that, "we learn more from failure than we do from success" holds true.

In this section we offer some possible remedies to common challenges you may encounter.

- ▶ Confronting Resistant Leaders
- ▶ Choosing Metrics That Matter
- ▶ Dealing with a Lack of Trust
- ▶ Ineffective and Unnecessary Meetings / Training
- ▶ Nine More Fixes and Tips

CONFRONTING RESISTANT LEADERS

"Dealing with employee issues can be difficult, but not dealing with them can be worse.

—Paul Foster, CEO The Business Therapist

In our story below, Chris happens to be a manager of a small manufacturing plant, but someone like Chris could be any person of influence in any role in any organization, from the frontline to the executive row. In fact, we find Chris everywhere!

The Problem With Chris

Chris is the plant manager of a small manufacturing site in the Midwest with about 150 employees running on three shifts. Chris has been the Plant Manager for over 15 years and no one dares challenge Chris' product knowledge or authority. The idea of a new, team-based work system, being ordered by top brass, did not appeal much to Chris. This plant has been making product profitably and Chris sees no reason to upset the applecart. More specifically, Chris is not going to let this new company program disrupt the operation. Command and control are what has worked to this point and Chris is not shy about sharing this philosophy.

Along with this new employee-engagement program comes a new CI position filled by a young person half Chris' age. Lee, full of enthusiasm and energy, has been promoted from the front-line ranks and is eager to begin the new job. Lee is knowledgeable of team dynamics, improvement tools, and processes. Lee connects well with the front-lines and appears to be the perfect choice for the CI role.

Chris feels the needs to teach this new recruit a few lessons about managing and explains to Lee, "we have tried this engagement stuff before; it may work down the street, but it won't work here. Besides, we don't have time to waste on listening to people gripe about how things are not fixed right and unresolved problems."

Lee tried very hard, but, over time, Chris pounded the enthusiasm and hope out of Lee. Other team members struggled to make things happen, but they were consistently blocked by Chris.

The saddest part of this true story is that the top management was very much aware of Chris' views and actions; they knew that Chris likely would never change. They hoped Lee's enthusiasm and connection to the rank and file could make a difference. Unsurprisingly, resistance prevailed.

The Real World

If this was an isolated case, we probably would have skipped this account entirely. Unfortunately, "Chris" exists in virtually every change effort. We do not attribute this fact to bad luck or timing, but rather to human nature and the challenge of implementing change.

What to Do?

Resistance is a pervasive challenge for every Continuous Improvement leader and it must be confronted, head-on. The survival of your improvement effort will depend on whether you overcome the resistance by person(s) with influence within your organization; therefore, thoughtful preparation and planning is required to deal with these influential resistors.

Borrowing a term from social media, an "influencer" is an individual or group with authority, expertise, or relationships that impact the decisions of others. On social media, influencers are high profile people – often celebrities – who can influence their thousands of followers to purchase a particular product or support a cause. They are often compensated for their influencing efforts. In our example, Chris' influence is negative, resisting a change initiative that would benefit the company.

Some influential resistors are high-profile, as in the case of Chris, the plant manager; but others can be found in any position. The characteristic that these resistors share with Chris is the ability to shape the attitudes and actions of their colleagues and team members. Some influential resistors cautiously stay underground, yet their colleagues clearly know where they stand. They may not say a word, but an eye roll or dismissive head toss is enough to signal to those they work with that this effort is not important - so don't take it too seriously.

Plant Manager Chris is a decent person, not really against improvements, but is busy with numbers to hit and an operation to run and fails to see how this new initiative could possibly help. Over the years, Chris was rewarded for kicking butt and taking names – Chris was good at it! This is the management style that Chris knows best and gets results – so why change?

As plant manager, Chris is an influencer and the resistance to the new vision must be confronted. Other managers and colleagues are watching to see whether Chris' approach or the new CI program will win out. Left unchallenged, Chris' authority and relationships will influence attitudes throughout the plant, undermining and possibly sinking the entire effort.

Confronting resistance is not easy, but the stakes are too high not to overcome it. We have found that the major reasons for failing to confront influential resistors are:

▶ It is politically unwise.

▶ Managers do not know how to effectively engage with resistors.

▶ They believe that it is hopeless.

▶ Conflict avoidance – takes courage.

The high cost of not confronting influential resistors:

▶ Puts the continuous improvement initiative at risk.

▶ Sustains a culture that lacks accountability.

▶ Provides unspoken approval.

▶ Loss of respect for those in charge.

▶ Fosters resentment.

▶ Undermines morale.

▶ It only gets worse.

Below is a model, we have employed for working with the influential resistors. It is built around mutual respect and establishing a dialogue to confront unacceptable behaviors. Over the years, we have assimilated and combined the work of several experts in the field of conflict and resolution. We have followed our model and know it works. We suggest the following approach to confronting resistant leaders:

The 5 Step Conversation

Step 1. Be Prepared

Always keep in mind that when a change effort is introduced, most of your colleagues will be assessing how the initiative affects them personally. Resistance is normal and to be expected.

▶ **Create a Win-Win:** Your conversation with the resistor should not be a win-lose discussion. Because this person has influence, it is in the best interest of the organization, the colleague, and you, as a CI leader, to persuade this person. *If unsuccessful, everyone loses.*

▶ **Show Respect:** Approach this conversation with respect for the individual and see your role as a peacemaker, not an enforcer. Plan a time and place that is convenient, provides privacy, and is without distractions. This meeting should be private and confidential.

▶ **See for Yourself:** If possible, it is very helpful to prepare by personally observing the behavior that is inconsistent with that which is desired. You need firsthand examples; hearsay is not acceptable.

▶ **Cite the Positives:** Also, take the time to note instances where this individual went above and beyond in support of the organization. Citing past examples of their good work can be helpful. Do not exaggerate or blow smoke, since this conversation must be honest and straightforward. Examples must be real or they will be regarded as manipulative.

Step 2. Call Out the Problem

Stating the problem accurately, enables both parties to begin to explore the possible causes and eventually seek solutions.

▶ **Do not Assume:** Your colleague may not be aware that their behavior is hampering improvement efforts.

▶ **Be Specific:** Describe observed behavior that is contrary to what is needed and expected. Explain how their behavior is affecting others and how it is detrimental

▶ **Acknowledging the Problem:** It is vital that your colleague recognizes and acknowledges that their behavior is creating a problem. Denial allows them to avoid responsibility and forestalls resolution. Once acknowledged, both parties can now begin to explore ways to resolve the problem.

Step 3. Share What You Know

Be honest and transparent. Explore the benefits to the organization, team, and the individual.

▶ **Start with the WHY:** Regardless of how well the initiative was communicated, do not assume that the person understands why the organization has embarked on this CI effort.

▶ **Describe the Benefits:** Be specific as to how the improvement helps the organization and how these changes will benefit them personally. If some gains have already occurred, share these "wins" with them.

▶ **Keep it simple.** Share with your colleague the likely changes and what will remain the same. Keep to the basics: What, How, Who and When.

Step 4. Listen to Understand

Resolution begins with understanding. Listen carefully what the other person is saying and what they really mean.

▶ **Be Curious:** Listen with a genuine sense of curiosity and not with a preconceived idea. Learn what they think and their concerns. Ask questions to enhance understanding, not to debate, but to learn.

▶ **Calm Fears:** While few are likely to admit it, remember that fear is the leading reason why people resist change. Fears of job loss, the unknown, and the future top the list. Fears are not the only reason for resistance, so listen carefully for other issues. If you can alleviate any of their fears do so, but do not mislead or sugarcoat anything.

Step 5. Map Out a Plan

Create a plan together. The plan must address the problems, be realistic and transparent.

▶ **Make clear the expectations:** What specifically are you requesting of your colleague?

▶ **Identify areas of agreement:** What can you agree on? Is there a basis on which you could move forward?

▶ **Develop a plan to act on the areas of agreement:** Use the areas of agreement as a bridge to resolving the matter. Commit to finding a way that will resolve the issue satisfactorily. Often, by tackling the issue together, new and better solutions are found. **Write the agreement out.**

▶ **Follow up:** Demonstrate your commitment by checking back with your colleague. Informal conversations by phone or over coffee can generate a positive outcome and ensure that progress is under way.

▶ **Plan an agreement review:** When will you meet again to formally review progress? If progress is not made and behaviors and attitudes reflect continued resistance, what happens next? No threats – just next steps.

What If Your Efforts Fail?

If you make a genuine, good-faith effort, and your resistors fail to get with the program, few options remain. If you leave an influential resistor in their current position, your efforts will be undermined either intentionally or by default. If this is the situation, they must be replaced.

In our true story above, Chris was finally replaced – unfortunately, three years too late. What we hear most often from top leadership when forced to replace an influential resistor – "we should have done it sooner."

👆 TAKEAWAYS

▶ "Influential resistors" exist in virtually every organization and change effort. The likelihood that you will encounter a "Chris" is almost a certainty.

▶ Because a "'Chris" has influence, and is overtly or covertly resistant to change, they must be confronted. There is no easy way and the stakes are high.

▶ A good-faith effort must be made to reach out to influential resistors. If successful, others with the same point of view are likely to come on board. If unsuccessful, more significant actions are required.

The Five Step Conversation with influential resistors template is available for download at www.thefivekeys.org

CHOOSING METRICS THAT MATTER

Metrics: quantitative measures to assess performance in achieving organizational goals and meeting customer and stakeholder requirements.

"If you cannot measure it, you cannot improve it"

**— Lord Kelvin,
Mathematical Physicist & Engineer**

oneyball: The Art of Winning an Unfair Game (Lewis 2003) was a book written by Michael Lewis and published in 2003, later made into a movie released in 2011. This true story of the 2002-2003 Oakland Athletics professional baseball team left an indelible impression on these CI practitioners.

In this true account, the management for the 2002 Athletics recognized that they could not attract top tier players given their limited payroll. For example, Major League Baseball annual team salaries in 2002, ranged from a low of $35 million to the high of $125 million. The A's player payroll in 2002 was the third lowest among the thirty teams in the League at $44 million.

Given this huge recruiting disadvantage, applying the traditional metrics associated with choosing and hiring the player with the greatest potential was a non-starter. Instead, the management determined the traditional player selection criteria of batting average, stolen bases, and runs batted in, was behind the times and through statistical analysis determined that on-base percentage and slugging percentage (an average of how many bases a player achieves per at bat) were actually better predictors of offensive success.

The A's applied this novel metrics formula guiding player recruitment and staying within their budget. The new player acquisition plan proved amazingly successful and the team went on to win the American League Division title in 2002 and 2003 allowing them to compete in the World Series both years.

Their success in applying these non-traditional metrics was extraordinary and the talk of the baseball world. Other teams soon began applying similar recruiting criteria competing for talent applying the A's formula.

We relate this story to provide a very non-traditional example of the impact the thoughtful selection of metrics can have on an organization. As the CI leader, you may have the opportunity to influence the selection of metrics — both leading indicators, those that will influence future results, as well as lagging indicators, those that confirm actual performance. The chart below provides an example of both, leading and lagging indicators in a variety of business settings.

What are Lagging and Leading Indicators?

Simply put, **lagging indicators** are a look in the rearview mirror documenting the results of past efforts. In terms of business operations, lagging indicators might be gross revenue, total volume, on-time delivery, overhead, employee turnover, etc. These results reveal trends and provide stakeholders with concrete evidence about how the organization has performed in the past.

Leading indicators are the opposite of lagging indicators. Leading indicators are actionable measures that strongly influence what is likely to occur in the future. These measures forecast probable results, in other words, the future lagging indicators. These measures might include customer satisfaction, improvements implemented, product development, number of new customers, etc. Most importantly, *leading indicators are actionable* – describing functions that are within the direct control of the organization.

Both lagging and leading indicators can provide valuable and essential functions in most organizations:

▶ Lagging indicators substantiate the well-being of the organization. They communicate to all stakeholders the critical performance results.

▶ Leading indicators provide insight about the likelihood of the organization achieving or surpassing their performance goals in the future.

It is obvious and necessary for organizations to focus on end results – those lagging indicators. Unfortunately, many organizations focus *solely* on those numbers. The result is a myopic view that neglects critical drivers that propel those bottom-line results.

Choosing the Right Indicators

Choosing lagging indicators is relatively easy (i.e., performance results important to stakeholders), while selecting leading indicators requires thoughtful consideration. Good leading indicators are those activities, functions, and actions over which you have control or influence that impact the critical performance measures. For example, if total revenue is a lagging indicator, then attaining new customers could be a leading indicator.

Generally, in most industries, adding new customers will lead to new revenue. More importantly, attaining new customers is an activity that the organization can impact through effort (research, marketing, sales), resources (people and data), and funding (salaries, advertising fees). Without effort, resources and adequate funding, the customer base likely will not expand and revenue will not increase. Conversely, devoting the necessary resources and funding to adding new customers will generate increased revenue. Adding new customers (a leading indicator) is, therefore, a viable predictor of future revenue (a lagging indicator). Identifying and prioritizing the appropriate leading indicators can dramatically improve the likelihood of meeting future performance goals.

Both leading and lagging indicators are appropriate and should align throughout an organization. Each function and department should have measures that indicate how they are contributing to their organization's strategy and performing against their goals (lagging indicators). Additionally, each function and department should have other measures that are actionable and will positively impact bottom-line financials.

The following table below provides examples of lagging and leading indicators spanning several industries.

Choosing Metrics

LAGGING INDICATORS		EXAMPLES	LEADING INDICATORS	
Analysis of Past Performance Results of What Has Been Done			Influence on Future Performance Predicts changes in the Organization	
Delivery Costs	On-Time Delivery	SUPPLIER	% of Perfect Orders	Backorder Rate
Average Sales per Store	Markdown Quantity	RETAIL	Average Sales per Basket	Markdown Amount
Injuries / Illness Rate	Total Lost Work Days	HEALTH / PRACTITIONERS	Number of Inspections	Safety and Health
Growth of Annual Sales	On-time Delivery	BUSINESS / SERVICES	Response Time	Process Availability
Gross Margin	Cost per Unit / Rush Orders	MANUFACTURING	Overall Equipment Effectiveness	Inventory Levels
Gross Revenue	Revenue per Customer	FOOD SERVICES	Customer Satisfaction	New Customers

TAKEAWAYS

► The "Moneyball" example describes the importance of thoughtfully choosing metrics that provide your organization with a competitive advantage.

► Lagging indicator convey past performance results. Leading indicators help predict future performance.

► Leading indicators are actionable – describing functions that are within the direct control of the organization.

DEALING WITH A LACK OF TRUST

"Trust is like the air we breathe – when it's present, nobody notices; when its absent, everybody notices."

— **Warren Buffett,**
CEO of Berkshire Hathaway

A trusting relationship between the Continuous Improvement leaders and their work colleagues is advantageous when launching change efforts. But what happens when a trusting relationship is not already established, and trust is low? What if colleagues don't know you? Perhaps you worked in another department, were a recent hire, or brought in as an external consultant. Maybe you have led past efforts that were not successful.

Many would argue that without the premise of trust, change initiatives are doomed to failure. Being able to count on one another to respond in predictable ways, they say, is a prerequisite to launching improvement efforts. Therefore, trust must be strong before launching improvement initiatives. *We disagree.*

In our experience, high levels of trust between management and front-line colleagues is often lacking as improvement programs are launched. Perhaps, even a history of traditional management practices has reinforced this paradigm. Past efforts may have upended longstanding practices that some find destabilizing and caused resentment. Resistance to change is always prevalent and the "lack of trust" provides some with justification to withhold support. Typically, colleagues prioritize their individual interests over the organization's needs. So, if trust is weak, do you move ahead? **Absolutely.** You can't wait for trust. Trust is a byproduct of doing hard things together.

The Benefits of Building Trust

Trust does not develop overnight, but making trust a hallmark of your continuous improvement culture will benefit your colleagues and support all aspects of the enterprise. (Atkinson 2017)

Trust within your organization:

▶ Opens communications.

▶ Encourages collaboration and teamwork.

▶ Establishes common goals.

▶ Increases the willingness to take risks.

▶ Allows for honest mistakes.

▶ Encourages colleagues to volunteer.

▶ Generates collaboration between departments.

▶ Allows accountability without fear.

▶ Improves morale.

▶ Reduces time in decision-making.

▶ Promotes candid and honest discussions.

▶ Diminishes resistance to change efforts.

How to Build Trust

Trust must be earned and, once earned, must be protected. In order to establish and maintain trust among your colleagues, the following actions are consequential in creating an environment of mutual trust. When leading continuous improvement efforts, "trust" means that colleagues can rely on you to:

▶ Speak the Truth – Be Honest and Open: Your integrity is paramount when it comes to leading. Keep your colleagues well informed. Explain your decisions and your rationale. Share the likely changes and what will remain the same. Level with them. Never mislead to soften the impact of the change effort. Your colleagues expect to be treated as peers and adults; therefore, you should provide them with reliable information.

▶ Lead by Example – Walk the Talk: Actions speak louder than words. Your behavior and that of other organization's leaders are constantly on display and scrutinized. Colleagues continually assess whether leaders genuinely practice the behaviors that they are advocating. If the leaders' walk does not match their talk, then it is unrealistic to expect others to follow.

▶ Be Predictable and Fair: Trust increases when colleagues know what to expect. No one is willing to go out on a limb if they think that it may get sawed off. Your consistent actions will build confidence among your colleagues to support your efforts. They will know that their commitment to the change will not be undercut or abandoned. Treat all your colleagues equally. Do not avoid assigning tasks to those who are resistant by choosing only those you believe you can count on. Demonstrate objectivity and fairness.

▶ Require Accountability: Holding people accountable, including yourself and other leaders, will create respect for you and confidence in the process. Adherence to completing tasks, meeting timelines, and providing honest assessments of progress or the lack thereof, will contribute significantly to your credibility and help establish a culture of transparency.

▶ Show Respect: Your colleagues have experience, wisdom and talent. Without them, and their contributions, no improvement effort will succeed. Recognize and respect them. Listen to what they have to say by seeking their input and advice. Be patient when colleagues are slower than others to adopt new practices, but challenge behaviors inconsistent with the culture you are building. Treat everyone as equals.

► Avoid Surprises: No one likes to be surprised. In the work environment, being surprised is inconsistent with good communications and embarrassing to those who are supposed to be aware. Knowing that the CI leader will keep colleagues well-informed and aware of relevant news will strengthen their relationships and ability to lead.

► Recognize Others - Share the Spotlight: You may be the CI leader, but successful change efforts require the contribution of many colleagues from throughout the organization. Do not hesitate to provide well-deserved acknowledgment of others' contributions. Recognition inspires commitment and the willingness to do even more. Everyone likes a pat on the back, as long as the recognition is deserved and authentic.

Finally, the building of real trust is a product of good leadership. Trust is built when people consistently do what they say they will do, time after time.

🖐️ TAKEAWAYS

► Build trust by demonstrating your trust in others.

► Don't let the lack of trust derail your improvement efforts.

► Make "trust" a hallmark of your continuous improvement culture.

INEFFECTIVE AND UNNECESSARY MEETINGS

"A manager's ability to turn meetings into a thinking environment is probably an organization's greatest asset."

— Nancy Kline, author

O ne of the most common complaints in every organization is that there are too many meetings – and that is before the introduction of a CI initiative. Time, like all other resources, is finite and must be shared among all the requirements and demands in the organization. As with any new initiative, some meetings, training, coaching and Q&A sessions will be required, thus adding to the time demands of other leaders and front-line colleagues. By planning and conducting effective meetings, you demonstrate that you respect their time and that you are a professional and the right person to lead the improvement effort.

Poorly run meetings waste colleagues' time and the organization's money; they are resented and often poorly attended.[53] In contrast, well-run meetings often are applauded and appreciated by attendees. Your best approach to gaining and maintaining support for the CI effort and providing defense against unneeded resistance is by adopting a meeting process that is responsive to your needs and respectful of the needs of your colleagues.

We recommend that you reacquaint yourself with good meeting design and practices, before hosting your first CI meeting. There are dozens of websites providing this advice and free templates

---

53   Martijn Aurik. Businesses waste $37 billion on ineffective meetings every year. What's your share? July, 2017. https://www.getminute.com/ineffective-meetings/

for planning and conducting effective meetings. We have found that the essentials commonly include:

Planning

▶ Choose a time, date and location that works for you and your colleagues.

▶ Create an invitation to the meeting and request attendance confirmation from your invitees.

▶ Circulate the invitation at least 7 days before the scheduled date.

▶ Your invitation should cover:

- Meeting Details: Time, place, and duration (**do not allow your meeting to exceed the allocated time**).

- Identify the host and list attendees.

- The purpose of the meeting.

▶ Request items others would like to add to the agenda.

The Agenda

▶ Unresolved items from the last meeting.

▶ New items for discussion.

▶ Actions to be taken / decisions to make.

▶ Communications, if any.

▶ Next Steps – Items for the next meeting.

▶ Future meeting - time and date.

Follow Up

Meeting Notes need not be extensive but capture:

▶ Highlights.

▶ Decisions made.

- ▶ Committed actions.

- ▶ Unresolved issues.

- ▶ Short summary.

- ▶ Next meeting time, date and venue.

Taking the time to plan and facilitate effective meetings demonstrates respect for your colleagues and commitment to the CI process.

🫴 TAKEAWAYS

The quality and effectiveness of your meetings are a direct reflection on your competency as the CI Leader.

The "Big Three" of productive meetings are:

- ▶ Planning

- ▶ The Agenda

- ▶ Follow-up

TRAINING COLLEAGUES

Training: teaching, or developing in oneself or others, any skills and knowledge that improves one's capability, capacity, productivity, and performance.

"The art of teaching is the art of assisting discovery."

— Mark Van Doren,
American Poet

In addition to ensuring that your meetings are well planned and executed as a CI Leader you are likely to host and conduct training sessions. The ability to create and deliver effective training is yet another skill set that should be honed and included in your personal "box of tools."

A most common requirement of CI leaders is to teach others. Disseminating the philosophies, tools, and methods of process improvement is what we do. While most of us have not had a formal teaching background, we know that your abilities in training your colleagues will have very direct impact on overall improvement results.

Our purpose here is not to provide a short course in how you train others but to highlight some key training aspects that we have found effective in our most successful training sessions.

Planning

1. **Establish training goals and outcomes**. Your training plans should align with the organization's vision and goals and the specific focus of the improvement initiative.

2. **Plan with the end in mind.** Identify what will be different because these training sessions were conducted. What are the specific deliverables?

3. **Create training sessions that are of short duration.** We find that shorter training sessions (approx. 2 – 3 hours) are more effective than all-day marathons.

4. **Accommodate different learning styles.** Plan your training session incorporating all three learning preferences:

   - **Visual Learning**: When information is presented visually. Seeing information helps to visualize concepts taught. (i.e. PowerPoint Slides, flip charts, workbooks, written questions, videos, etc.)

   - **Auditory Learning**: When information is presented in an auditory manner. Hearing information helps to internalize concepts taught. Discussions, videos, lectures, music and podcasts

   - **Kinesthetic Learning**: When information is presented kinesthetically. Using hands/bodies and action helps to experience the concepts taught. Group exercises, brainstorms, games, activities, and field trips.

     Being prepared with an array of different methods of presenting your material honors the different learning styles of your attendees.

5. **Prepare your materials** and equipment, for each segment of training, well in advance.

Training Day

1. Inviting a senior level representative to kick off the session demonstrates commitment to the effort and adds some level of accountability. A good start.

2. Begin with the "WHY." Explain to your session members what will be presented to them and why this training is important, how it benefits the organization and those being trained.

3. List and explain the objectives for the session. Each trainee should know what is about to be presented and what they are about to learn.

4. Make training interactive. Group discussions and problem-solving energize trainees. Include exercises and videos. Consider having participants work in pairs or table teams.

5. Avoid "death by PowerPoint." When using PowerPoint slides, create interactive discussions. Don't read the slides.

6. Always assign homework. Reinforce what has been taught by assigning small tasks that embeds the learning for each trainee - "homework" can be presented by participants at the next session.

7. If specific follow-up tasks are required, ensure each trainee is clear on the expectations. Create a visual record of what and who.

8. Always start and finish on time.

Evaluations

Every training session should conclude with a short, written evaluation. This brief activity is not a critique of the training session design nor the presenters.

Evaluations accomplish three main functions:

1. Demonstrates respect for the opinions and advice of participants.

2. Requires the participants to personally reflect on what they have learned and experienced and can highlight the benefits.

3. Helps ensure the purpose of the training is being realized and can provide helpful advice for future training sessions. Additionally, the feedback provides a tangible record of progress being made.

The short list of *open-ended questions* requires participants to think about their responses and is not a "check the box" exercise. Good feedback contributes to even better training sessions.

NOTE: Do Not Take Feedback Personally. Each participant is expressing what they are feeling in the moment, so accept their responses simply as data: *nothing more – nothing less.*

CI Training in a nutshell:

Training the Why? Employees must understand why the improvement initiative is important to the organization and how it connects to the vision and what it means to them personally.

People can't do what they don't understand – Whatever improvement tools your organization chooses to utilize, employees must have a sound understanding of **How** and **When** to use them. (i.e., problem solving , Kaizen, 5S, whatever!)

> **Foster Success!** – Now that employees understand the Why, How, and When, provide the opportunities for improvement to take place. Continued coaching and reward and recognition provide opportunities to reinforce new behaviors.

Other Advice

Becoming an effective trainer/teacher takes time and commitment. Mastering the materials, reading your audience, learning when to pose questions, generate discussions and debate, expand on concepts, or move on to new material requires experience and timing. Maintaining a flexible agenda allows for that freedom to read the audience and make adjustments for the most impact. It is rare that two training sessions are identical!

In our experience, the very best teachers/trainers:

▶ Create a safe learning environment.

▶ Create a positive experience, building on what the trainees already know.

▶ When possible work in pairs. Two experienced trainers, can support each other and provide additional insight and flexibility.

▶ Can read their audience and pivot for most engagement and learnings (breaks, closing discussions, pursuing a valid point, shifting agenda).

▶ Know when to lead the group and when to be neutral in order to achieve desired outcomes.

▶ Is steadfast in their focus on achieving the *Purpose of the session.*

Perhaps, the most valuable lesson learned from my mentors is the value of understanding the purpose of my work. If it is a facilitation session, the place to start for me is to ask "What is the purpose of this facilitation session? What are the outcomes? What will be different at the end of the day?" By going through this exercise, I become much clearer on what it is I have to do that day. By keeping true to the session's purpose and the principles of how people learn in mind, the agenda often writes itself.

TAKEAWAYS

▶ A most common requirement of CI leaders is to teach others.

▶ The ability to create and deliver effective training is a skill set that should be honed and included in your personal "box of tools."

▶ Always provide written evaluation forms to participants at the end of each training session.

A Workshop Evaluation template is available for download at www.thefivekeys.org

NINE MORE FIXES AND TIPS

Unrealistic Expectations for Frontline Leaders

The unsung heroes of continuous improvement work are on the front lines. These leaders, both supervisors and team leaders, combine with their colleagues to implement changes to their process and their work habits. These colleagues overcome their own fears of change and lead others in problem solving and implementing improvements.

Sometimes, the expectations for these leaders is unrealistic and unrewarded. While leading the team is their work, it is unfair to expect these individuals to be responsible for all that happens on the front line, both good and bad. Nor is it realistic to expect these individuals will have all the answers and solutions at the moment problems surface. Treat these colleagues well and recognize their many accomplishments. They are your greatest resource!

Accountable Without Authority

A common dilemma often emerges as you recruit respected colleagues to take the lead in ongoing improvement initiatives. Typically, team members are chosen to head up an initiative and, subsequently, held accountable for outcomes. Yet, the corresponding authority necessary for the individual to carry this task out and ensuring action, is withheld – usually without intention.

The likely result is the lack of progress, frustration for the task leader, and reluctance of colleagues to be placed in this position. To depend solely on one's ability to coax and cajole their colleagues to follow their lead is unrealistic and untenable. You need all the supporters you can get, and therefore, must provide them with the "tools" necessary to perform the requested tasks.

To avoid a "straw boss" scenario that spawns jealousy or resentment, carefully consider the amount of authority required to perform the task. It will be necessary to consistently coach the individual on the use of this limited authority. Also, it will be helpful to encourage other leaders and managers to provide your agent with the assistance and tools necessary for task completion. Finally, broadly communicating the role of this "project leader" and those who will be working with them will pave the way for understanding and support.

Never Make Assumptions

Continuous Improvement efforts are usually accompanied by management's willingness to share business data with the front-line employees. Once the province of "managers only," all types of relevant information is made available to colleagues across the organization. This transparency is significant and represents a real shift from traditional management practices to those aligned with continuous improvement. Front-line employees, both supervisory and operations, are now trusted with proprietary information and recognized as valued team members enlisted in the search for improvements.

While signaling a bright new era, we have often observed that the presentation of certain information leaves participants scratching their heads. While understood in the board room, today's business lexicon presents an assortment of unfamiliar terms, acronyms, metrics, flow charts, diagrams, bar graphs and pie charts with an x-axis and y-axis, etc. to a bewildered audience. While this scenario is common, rarely will a meeting attendee openly admit a lack of understanding or request an explanation.

CI leaders must recognize that specialized or technical data may be unfamiliar and confusing to the uninitiated. Take the time to regularly define terms and acronyms, establish a common vocabulary, and thoroughly explain graphs and charts and what they show. Do not assume that your colleagues know. Establish a safe learning environment where it is comfortable for colleagues to ask questions.

Home Runs Versus Base Hits

We all know that the fundamental principle of Continuous Improvement is a focus on implementing small incremental improvements over time. Despite the obvious advantages of small improvements (requiring less cost, risk, time, etc.) versus the "game changer" (requiring greater cost and taking bigger risks), senior leaders are continually pressed to deliver the "breakthrough innovation" to the organization's stakeholders. Unfortunately, this demand is often counterproductive.

For example, a process redesign may be viewed as a "game changer," however, statistics show that the compounding effects of incremental improvements, over time, will generate far greater bottom line results without the risks and resource demands of a major overhaul.

Don't Throw It Over the Wall

Launching a CI initiative will generate an avalanche of improvement ideas from the front lines. Once your colleagues learn that the effort is real, there is no holding back their enthusiasm and steady flow of good ideas. The old saying "be careful what you wish for" may come to mind as you sort through the neck-deep pile of suggestions, some feasible, some not.

We have learned to prepare for this onslaught by developing a process for assessing and implementing improvement ideas well in advance of a program launch.

The six aspects of an effective improvement process are:

1. Capturing improvement ideas and utilizing visual management of improvements.

2. Assessment of impact – pros and cons – needs and feasibility.

3. Approval or Rejection Process – responding back to idea sponsors.

4. Implementation – PDCA cycle.

5. Reward and Recognition of implemented ideas.

6. Assess whether the improvement can be implemented in other areas?

Another implementation method we like is the "just-do-it" approach. If the individual or team recommends an improvement that is subsequently approved, and they have the ability to safely implement the improvement, then they are authorized to move ahead and "just-do-it." No delay – just get it done!

Request for Help - Bring in the Pros

One common scenario that inhibits the "just-do-it" approach is that the improvement idea sponsor(s) lacks the skill set or authority necessary to make the required changes. Some improvements may necessarily be handed off to a different department, perhaps Human Resources, Maintenance, Information Technology, etc., or even an outside supplier. At this juncture, implementation becomes more complicated. Each of these departments has their own ongoing responsibilities, priorities, funding, and staffing issues, as well as bureaucracies to navigate.

Recognize that the timeline for implementation may become unpredictable. These delays frequently cause friction among interest groups when the implementation timeline slips. This unpredictability can lead to colleagues becoming disillusioned while providing CI naysayers with evidence that "this stuff is just talk." *Inoculate your colleagues by acknowledging this probability and forewarning them before expectations become entrenched. This is the real world and a level of unpredictability is to be expected.*

Lack of a Designated CI Person

Many organizations are too small or cannot afford to employ an individual solely focused on continuous improvement. This is an unfortunate, yet real issue. While it is true that continually improving is everyone's job, someone still needs to spearhead initiatives and steer the process to that end. If this is your situation, give thoughtful consideration to who is the spearhead and how that individual can be supported.

Finding Needed Supporters

In organizations with a flat structure and limited resources, the site leader often becomes the default CI leader. These individuals typically have the authority to assign projects to staff and require accountability. The primary challenge in smaller organizations is not will or ability to tackle improvement efforts; rather, it is lack of available staff time. Regardless of the backdrop, the need to continually improve is not going away and waiting for more staff and resources is a poor option.

We have found that creating an improvement "steering group" consisting of influential staff and front-line colleagues can help offset some deficits in manpower and time demands. Engaging others in identifying improvement opportunities, developing plans together for implementation and rotating project responsibilities among several colleagues can minimize work overload and maintain needed support.

Without a "full-time" CI leader, improvement efforts likely will advance at a slower pace, but progress can be made by creating a larger pool of project owners and spreading tasks among more colleagues. If your colleagues are truly a part of the planning, and additional duties and responsibilities are fairly shared, these efforts are likely to be successful.

A Picture Is Worth A Thousand Words - Ford Rouge Plant

Bringing change to a static, mature worksite requires additional planning and effort. With each day that passes, the prevailing culture within that organization becomes more entrenched. Change does not come easy and with many improvement efforts, some changes in the culture (work habits) are required.

This account details how helping others see what the changes actually entail, made the difference between success and failure.

From 1990-1997 , I was the leader of United Auto Workers (UAW) Local Union 600 representing some 10,000 members in the Ford Rouge Plant. The Rouge, a strident change-averse environment, consisted of several distinct manufacturing operations ranging from steelmaking to auto assembly.

At the time, the Rouge Engine Plant desperately needed a new replacement engine model to remain a viable manufacturing site for Ford. Ford had several engine manufacturing plants located around the world that could produce this new engine; each of these sites was more efficient and cost competitive then the Rouge.

For the Rouge Engine Plant to be awarded this new product, significant and substantial changes in work practices were required. Not surprisingly, resistance to change was intense and shared by many plant employees, union leaders, and company officials.

To demonstrate the necessity for making these changes, Ford and the UAW arranged for key union leaders and management staff to visit four Ford engine manufacturing facilities. During these site visits, union leaders and Ford managers explored together the newer manufacturing processes and work practices employed there. Seeing these more up to date approaches to engine manufacturing and meeting the various management and union groups at these other sites enlightened our discovery team. By observing, first-hand, the changes that were necessary to remain competitive, the pathway to implementation was provided to both management and union leaders. The parties agreed on the changes necessary and the new engine was awarded to the Rouge Engine Plant.

We relate this true example of *a picture being worth a thousand words* to demonstrate the value of seeing and experiencing what certain changes look like for management and employees. If your improvement or change initiative is major, consider visiting a similar venue that has implemented the change. If a visit is not practical, invite a knowledgeable spokesperson from the site to meet with your team, share advice and describe lessons learned. Helping others "to see" can accelerate your initiative.

Measure Behavior Change for Improvement and Sustainment

As new behaviors are integrated into the daily/weekly/and monthly work routines, it is a good practice to identify metrics to quantify these new behaviors. Because behaviors reflect the culture of an organization, corresponding measures are benchmarks for progress, identify opportunities for coaching, define next steps, and link rewards and recognition.

Typical performance measures such as Quality, Throughput, and Cost-effectiveness can reflect behavioral changes; the following list provides examples of added drivers in the development of a continuous improvement worksite culture.

Problem solving actions	Safety hazards identified
Root causes identified	Reward and recognition opportunities
Reoccurring problems eliminated	Coaching sessions
Kaizen projects	Six Sigma projects completed
5S audits	Updated SOPs
PDCAs completed	Improvement ideas implemented

🖐️🎁 TAKEAWAYS

Each of us, engaged in continuous improvement, accumulates over time, an array of antidotes to access when problems arise.

These 9 we keep, at the ready, and hope you will find them beneficial in your work.

SECTION 4

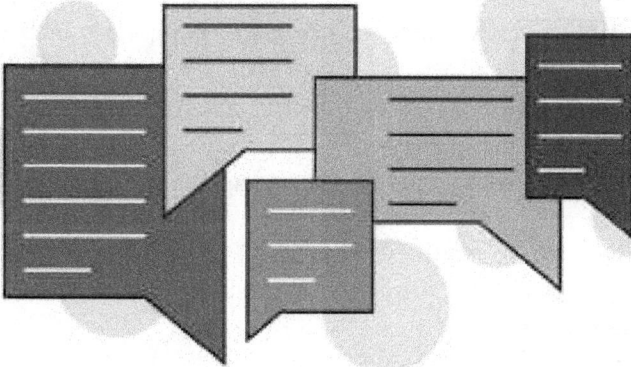

SHARE YOUR STORY

I n this section, we share five perspectives from well-respected colleagues working in geographically-scattered locations. Each has worked in the continuous improvement arena for decades – however their field of play is very different.

This is what they had to say in responding to the query: **"What have you learned through personal experience that you wish to share with other CI leaders?"**

George Byrne's experience spans multiple continents and industries as a principal consultant for major corporations (Caterpillar Inc., The LG Group, Johnson & Johnson, British Petroleum) as well as, being an executive level implementor of continuous improvement.

Rosa Zapata specializes in organizational change and business transformation. She has assisted varied industries, mining companies and academic institutions throughout Latin America from Mexico to Argentina.

Dr. Ian Matheson has shared with legions of managers on six continents his experience and structured approaches to boosting bottom-line performance and assisting companies in becoming truly great places to work. He is presently based in Johannesburg, South Africa.

Kevin Boyle works with labor/ management groups in Europe, Mexico, and the United States as they pursue continuous improvement initiatives. Forming alliances, implementing strategies, and transforming relationships is the heart of these change efforts.

Marcos Pavani is a civil engineer who has been leading continuous improvement teams, in Brazil, for over twenty years.

► Sustainability - George Byrne

► The Four Gremlins – Rosa Zapata

► The Power of Visual Management – Ian Matheson

► Continuous Improvement: Inside the Farm Gate – Kevin Boyle

► Focus on the Vision – Marcos Pavani

SUSTAINABILITY

GEORGE BYRNE
Nictom Consulting Group

Our personal journey with continuous improvement (CI) in organizations has run the gamut from being the person in charge of a CI effort to being consultants to C-suite executives in major organizations and multiple industries around the world. We've been fortunate to have had both good and some not-so-good experiences. The good experiences helped us to learn what worked and what didn't work; the not-so-good experiences taught us lessons about people, processes, and culture that might seem obvious, but oftentimes are not.

It's rather easy to start a continuous improvement initiative in most organizations. Often there's a burning platform, a call to action, a need to transform the organization. The myriad of reasons to launch CI include competitive market dynamics, ever-increasing customer demands, industry economics, technology undercurrents, and even something as unassuming yet significantly important as workforce efficiency and effectiveness.

But in hindsight, after over 30 years in the CI trenches, we still find that one of the biggest challenges is sustaining the effort once it has launched. Our experience has shown that the initial euphoria, depending on the organization, will last anywhere from 3 months to a year. The danger lies in the initiative eventually being viewed as just another program of the day or flavor of the month.

There is plenty of information in this book dealing with the direct correlation between leadership and success of the initiative. And in our heart, we believe that most leaders of CI initiatives start out with great intentions. However, most don't go into it thinking about long-term sustainability. A focus on immediate results drives this behavior; and while results are definitely important, leaders should also be thinking from the start about how to keep it going. How do I make it become part of the DNA of my organization?

And this is one of the things that we've been told by some leaders that they wish they had known early on in their role as a CI leader. That is, how can they make this not just a part of what they do every day, but make it last.? How do they get to the point where CI is ingrained in the organization in such a way that it becomes a habit rather than a task?

Looking at best practices from organizations with a successful history of CI, one can see some commonalities that drove both short-term results and long-term success:

▶ Leaders in these successful organizations view CI not just from the technical implementation perspective, but more from a people and change management perspective. There are plenty of books and roadmaps out there that will show any number of approaches and frameworks for a CI deployment. They'll provide a leader with somewhat nebulous timelines along with step-by-step, specific actions or tasks that should be undertaken. They'll also espouse philosophies with well-known and branded methodologies from successful organizations. But the key, the real key, to sustainment is to take the approach that a leader thinks would work best and to make it personal for the people in her or his organization. Without buy-in from the heart and brains of the organization, and its people, CI can never be sustained over the long term.

▶ CI efforts tailored to suit the needs of individual business units or work locations avoid the cookie-cutter approach to deployment and implementation. Said another way: one-size-fits-all rarely works in complex organizations. The variables that need to be cared for are just too varied.

People are different by nature. Suppliers and vendors with input to processes may vary. And even various customer segments may have different needs and wants. So, are we saying that it's OK to get away from proven best practices and techniques when a leader deploys CI? Absolutely not! Think of baking a chocolate cake. While there are some basic ingredients that are absolutely necessary, each baker may take a different approach to how the cake is actually prepared and baked. The same is true with CI deployment in organizations. Yes, there are some basic ingredients that you absolutely must have for long-term success. But it's OK to launch and to deploy CI in a way that fits your organization if the basic ingredients for success are included.

▶ Performance scorecards are used not just to display results and to celebrate successes. Rather, they are used to facilitate staff meetings and to make decisions on where to go next. This approach ensures that the overall operating system of the organization is fully aligned to drive improvements and to execute strategies. Long-term sustainment of a CI initiative requires that leaders look forward. Using scorecards or data simply to look in the rear-view mirror does nothing other than to tell you how you've done. The more pressing question for leaders is how are you going to perform in the future? How are you going to adapt to the evolving demands of your customers and the markets that you serve? Do your people have the right skills sets and tools to execute the strategies that you've asked them to work toward?

▶ World class organizations go from building short-term compliance to long-term commitment. And the leaders in these organizations understand that CI is most effective when the rank and file, the people toiling day in and day out to meet organizational objectives, are given the tools, direction, and empowerment to make things better.

Leaders have told us that CI can be somewhat of a quandary. That is, launching an initiative is not hard. With the right tools given to employees, with the inclusion of best practices and ingredients for success, and with the right mindset, CI is usually bought into immediately by most people in most organizations. And there will be some immediate results that warrant celebration. The hard part is sustaining it.

So, how can a leader sustain CI? This is where leaders must look beyond the textbook frameworks and the initial success stories that they'll undoubtedly have. This is where leaders must make a personal commitment to not just delegate but to be visibly involved in CI training and projects. This is where leaders show that they are in it for the long haul and that they will support front-line efforts to improve efficiency and effectiveness. This is the time to avoid the obvious and to dig deep for answers to complex questions that will arise. This is the time for leaders to show that CI is part of their personal DNA.

Long term sustainment of CI is never guaranteed. But leaders must take ownership for it to happen.

THE FOUR GREMLINS

ROSA ZAPATA
CDI Latin America

Introduction

There are many challenges to be faced on the continuous improvement road. Those who decide to embark on this journey for the sake of their businesses, organizations, or associations, must have the skill of identifying them and having a plan on hand to mitigate their effects as soon as possible. Otherwise, progress might be at risk.

As consultants, we are called to provide advice, to coach, and to share our experience and skills with the organization´s leadership. We are given the opportunity to work with them, but also to learn from them and the way they make final decisions once the advice, coaching, and experience is shared. This is an iterative process with each party learning from the other. Many of those decisions are highly related to the challenges mentioned above and how they will be tackled.

During my years as a consultant, I have witnessed similar challenges appear regardless of the industry or sector the company is in. These common challenges show themselves at different stages of the continuous improvement journey and they do not differentiate between strategic, systemic, or operational teams. Their mission is to retard progress and they are mostly individual or company behavior related.

I call them *The Four Gremlins*[54], and they must be kept at bay.

Gremlin 1: Silo

"Silos" describe an organizational environment where knowledge and information are not shared, thereby establishing separation and isolation between functions.

The ideal conditions for gremlin Silo to appear are when each team member has his/her own interpretation of the objective(s), which must be achieved by the team (see figure 13).

There might be different reasons for this to happen, ranging from the need for better discussion leading to a more explicit team vision and/or purpose to the fact that maybe more cohesion in the leadership team is required. Regardless of the reason, the usual effect of this silo mindset is misalignment throughout the organization, fire fighting amongst business units, absence of achievable targets that enable the whole organization to move forward, disappointed employees and customers, stress and more. This is why the conditions that make gremlin Silo strong must be identified and tackled from the beginning.

Although the existence of gremlin Silo might sound obvious, I am surprised how often I find it meddling with the good work of well-intentioned managers who want to move their organizations to a world-class mindset. There are different mechanisms to assess how clear to each team member the objective is and, most importantly, whether or not it is perceived as a common goal and the role each member should play. Clarity in the organization starts with clarity in the management team.

---

54 According to the Oxford dictionary a gremlin is a folkloric mischievous creature regarded as responsible for unexplained malfunctions in aircraft or other machinery.

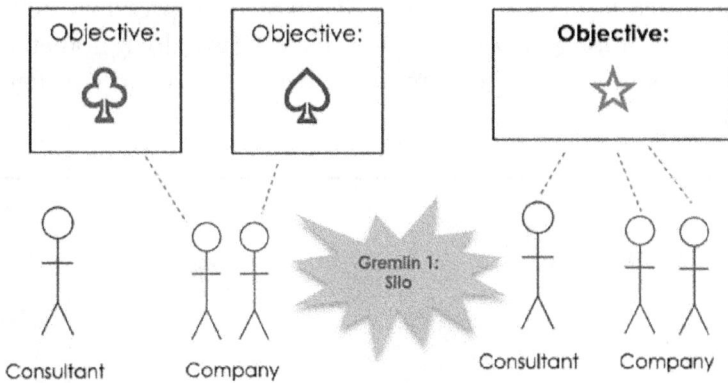

Figure 13. Usually team members have different interpretations of the objectives desired. The role of a CI leader is to promote the necessary discussion so the team members agree on a "common image" of what the goal is. This helps to strengthen cohesion and trust not only amongst team members but also with the consultant or CI champion whose role is to help them.

Gremlin 2: Inertia

In physics[55], inertia is a property of matter by which it continues in its existing state of rest or uniform motion in a straight line, unless that state is changed by an external force. And, according to the Oxford dictionary[56], it is a tendency to do nothing or to remain unchanged.

Once the team has a common picture of what they want to achieve, actions for moving forward are agreed upon, and this is the moment when gremlin Inertia usually strikes. In a business environment, Inertia shows itself in the form of *inaction*; in simpler words, it is when a team member does not do what he/she

---

55   www.merriam-webster.com/dictionary/inertia.
56   Oxford English Dictionary. Oxford University Press; Edition: 7 (2012).

committed to do for the team. Alternatively, it presents itself in the form of *doing not-agreed actions*, which means, doing something that does not move the team in the desired direction (see figure 14).

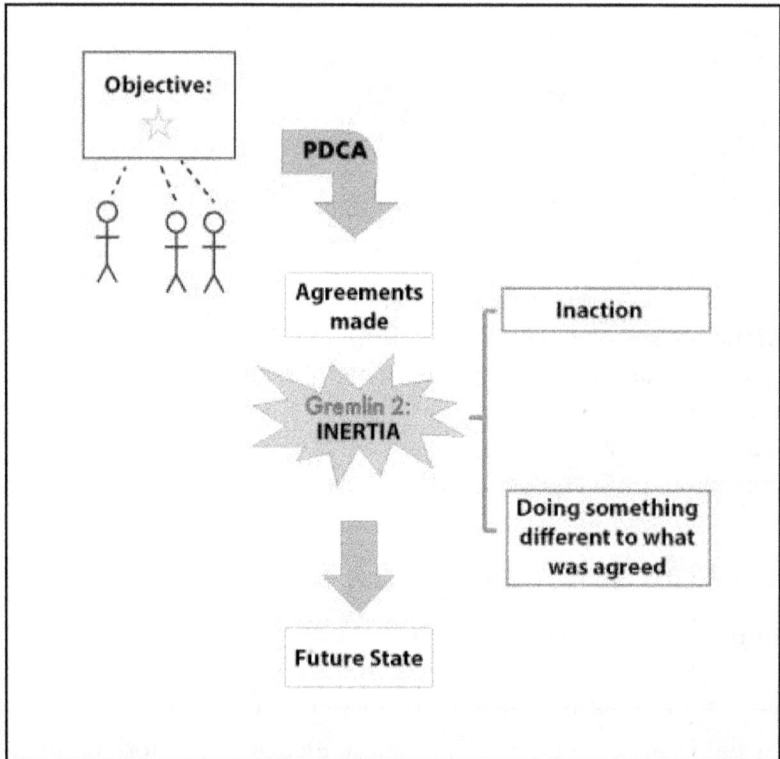

Figure 14. The two ways inertia is present on a continuous improvement journey.

Having a common objective does not mean that everyone is moving at the same speed to achieve it. Inaction flourishes in the absence of a sense of urgency, as explained by Mr. John Kotter in his book,[57] and particularly, when the day-to-day activities drown

---

57   John Kotter *A Sense of Urgency*. (Cambridge: Harvard Business Review Press; 2008.)

the long-term priorities. It does not help either when there are no clear roles or accountabilities in the team.

On the other hand, not-agreed actions are usually the result of old habits or behaviors like planning in a traditional way, when the agreed action is not fully understood but there is not a sufficient level of trust within the team to makes them comfortable to ask questions or challenge a specific action yet, or it is just an expression of a passive resistance to change.

To defeat inertia in the team, a truthful, active, and visible leadership is required to drive teamwork, to keep each other accountable, to raise standards, and to eliminate shallow harmony. A path to develop a healthy leadership that supports the organization strategy is a must. After all, teamwork is the ultimate competitive advantage.

Gremlin 3: Disconnect

When introducing a new initiative, particularly one of continuous improvement, it is critical to consider the effort in its entirety not individual elements. Gremlin Disconnect appears, when the connection is lost between each facet of the initiative.

When segments of a continuous improvement initiative are tackled as a singular effort, certain important aspects of that project are often left unsettled. For example, when implementing new software, this could mean ensuring that the software is customized to meet the business needs. (*project management*)

However, it is not enough to consider the technical elements to the project only. It is necessary to manage the people side as well (*change management*). Understanding how people react to change and having a plan to help them cope with it is key to the success of any project. People react differently to change and this ultimately determines the speed at which the organization fully embraces the new initiative.

There is another aspect to consider. . . The progress made on both the technical side and the people side of the project requires an active and visible leadership from those interested in bringing the change to the organization (see Figure 15). *Active and visible leadership* means not avoiding the uncomfortable conversations needed to create a sense of urgency, facilitating the needed resources to go through the change, building trust, and promoting clear roles and accountability during the process. It also means giving recognition as loudly as possible to those who are moving faster on the acceptance and mastery of the change in order to give living examples of how the future state looks. It also provides a fine way of building the new culture by celebrating success.

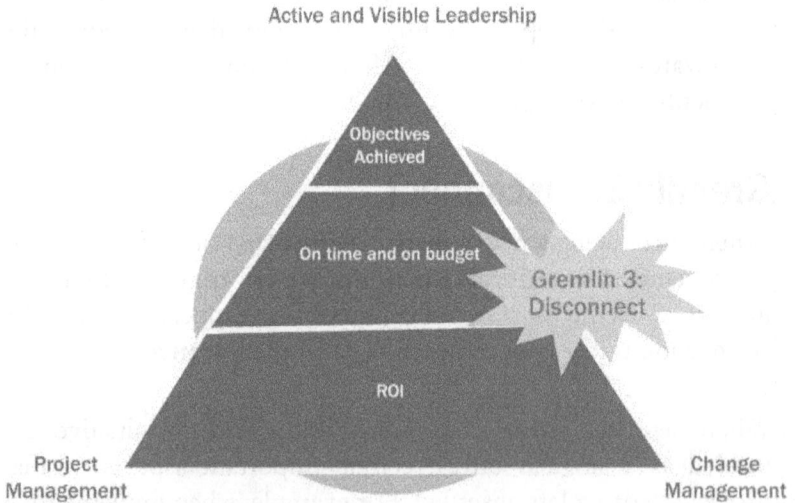

Active and Visible Leadership

Objectives
Achieved

On time and on budget

Gremlin 3:
Disconnect

ROI

Project
Management

Change
Management

Figure 15. Three elements for a successful continuous improvement journey.

Gremlin 4: Skepticism

"Give me a lever long enough and a fulcrum on which to place it, and I shall move the world."

- Archimedes.

Regardless of the continuous improvement methodology used, if there are not enough people behind that methodology, seeing the benefit of it, supporting it, understanding it, practicing it and helping others, it may not last long.

This number of people is called "critical mass." They are a force within the organization strong enough to neutralize any attempt to go back to the old ways from those who follow Gremlin Skepticism and do not see a real need to change, particularly when their previous behaviors or beliefs helped them to be successful at some point in their careers, I like to think of those advocates for change as a "lever" in the organization (see Figure 16).

It helps to keep under control the Silo, Inertia, and Disconnect mindset to create a large enough critical mass. At the end of the day, we are talking about improving the organizational culture and every person´s involvement is needed.

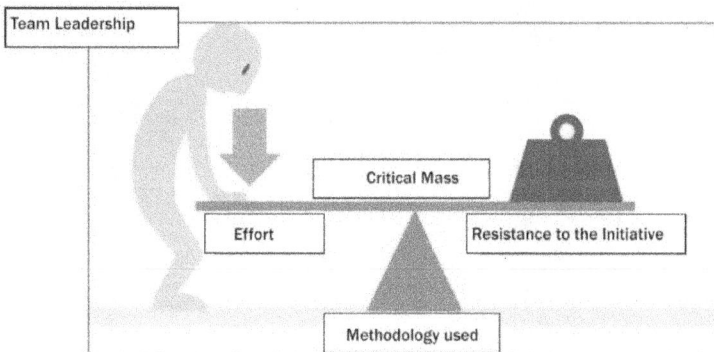

Figure 16. The bigger critical mass is, the faster the change will be accepted and mastered.

Ideas for Reflection

▶ Clarity in the organization starts with clarity in the management team.

▶ A successful continuous improvement initiative is based on three basics: an active and visible leadership, a change management process, and a project management approach.

▶ Inaction and doing not-agreed actions are forms of inertia in the organization.

▶ A key aspect of the change management process is to work towards achievement of critical mass.

LEVERAGING THE POWER OF VISUAL MANAGEMENT

DR. IAN MATHESON
CDI - Africa-Middle East-Americas

This article examines certain human elements that differentiate success and failure in the workplace. The focus is not to introduce new process tools and techniques, but explore successful leadership behaviors.

One key differentiator is Skill. Lewis Hamilton could probably navigate the Monaco Grand Prix circuit faster in a MiniCooper than the average motorist driving Hamilton's high performance Mercedes. A skilled coach will have significantly greater success than a novice. A skilled leader will address conflict, handle under-performance, recognise exceptional performance, promote worker engagement and so much more better than a novice.

So what can we do as continuous improvement facilitators to enable the managers to deliver at a higher level? One important learning that we can share is the power of visual management (a method to visually communicate) as our ally in the quest. If the message is succinct, the power is immense.

Young schoolchildren are rewarded with gold or silver stars for good performance, sometimes even applied to their foreheads when they leave at the end of classes. The top performers are sometimes given notices to put on the window of their parent's car to show that they have excelled. These visual indicators trigger a virtuous cycle, prompting the child to continue the fine efforts. The skill of the teaching staff is required to ensure that under-performers continue to be motivated to improve.

In business, we employ exactly the same practices. Many workplaces display images of their top performers as recognition. I have visited sites in the Philippines and Japan where an image of a racetrack was displayed in the workplace. Every team member was allocated a separate lane and his/her marker was moved forward every time one of their suggestions was implemented. There was spirited competition to find innovative solutions to the business challenges.

Negative performance can be similarly highlighted. Action not completed by a due date can be made prominent. Persistent late-comers at meetings can be indicated, with a view to motivating them to make a little more effort to arrive on time.

The benefit of visual tools, such as these, is that one is presenting *facts* and not simply the view of the leader. A leave chart will show who wishes to take leave on particular days, and if a minimum number of people are required to operate the business, it becomes clear that only a specific number may be absent at any time. The team leader is not required to make a decision that a team member cannot take time off during a heavy vacation period.

Of course, the ultimate visual measures of performance are the graphs presenting KPIs. Here, certain rules apply. Visuals must be simple to understand. They must track lead and not lag indicators, so that the team is empowered to influence the outcome. Members must know that management is there to assist them when they struggle to make target. They come to know that "a Failure is a Treasure," i.e. a learning opportunity to do better in future, and that this is understood by management.

The benefit of visual tools, such as these, is that one is presenting facts and not simply the view of the leader.

Managers play a key role in assisting the team in identifying good measures. Sales volume is a common, but rather ordinary measure. Maybe better targets may be sales visits, response time to inquiries, or delivery lead times, which then in turn may impact on sales volume, a lag indicator. Number of accidents is another ordinary measure. Measurement of near misses, job safety observations, or even scheduling of informative interactive awareness sessions may be more appropriate for front-line personnel. Number of units processed or produced per day is ordinary. A little problem-solving exercise could take the team closer to the "magic button" which impacts on final results. This could be changeover times, maintenance schedule completion rates, or even the time the process was up and running at the start of the day. The lag measures are still of critical importance and must be tracked, but the real focus of attention is on charting progress of the key driver(s). When performance is recorded in a physical file or computer spreadsheet, we are effectively measuring performance, but the role of the team is to manage performance. This can be so much more effective when performance is immediately visible.

Today, all team members are encouraged to be actively engaged in the business. In order to do so, they must have their manager's support, clearly understand the organization's vision and objectives and their role in helping achieve them. Providing colleagues with current performance feedback and the resources they require enables them to meet expectaions. When expectations are met, appropriate recognition should be awarded. None of these aspects flows automatically from the visual tool. Each must be carefully delivered by a transparent empathetic leader.

Visual management can prove to be a powerful tool, yet is only one of many in today's vast improvement arsenal. In our role as continuous improvement specialists, we are the catalyst for continued learning and growth, assisting leaders in becoming more effective and utilizing the power of the tools at their disposal.

1. Putwain. Lean Management Journal. 9 June 2015.

2. Szwejczewski & Marsh. Cranfield Univ. School of Management. March 2012

CONTINUOUS IMPROVEMENT: INSIDE THE FARM GATE

KEVIN BOYLE

Equitable Food Initiative

For over four decades, I have led continuous improvement efforts with various organizations in the US, Europe and Mexico. During this last decade however, I have focused primarily on working with the men and women in the U.S. produce industry.

American produce encompasses a huge swath of US agriculture delivering fresh and processed fruits and vegetables to dinner tables across the country. In the US, the fruit and vegetable market was valued at $104.7 billion in 2016. This figure is expected to reach $1.1 trillion by 2025, according to a report by Grand View Research, Inc.[58] As for employment, estimates vary. According to experts, there are approximately 2.5 million to 3 million farmworkers (NCFH 2018) and another ½ million retail jobs associated with the industry.[59]

---

58 Grand View Research. U.S. Fruit & Vegetables Market Size, Share & Trends Analysis Report 2018-2025. 2018

59 Tamar Haspel. "In an Immigration Crackdown, Who Will Pick OurProduce?" *Washington Pos.*, March 17, 2017. https://www.washingtonpost.com/lifestyle/food/in-an-immigration-crackdown-who-will-pick-our-produce/2017/03/17/

Global Industry

The American produce industry operates in a global economy with relatively free trade. This status permits unbridled competition from lower-wage countries, some with minimal regard for health and safety measures, competing directly for American consumers. Today's challenges to compete and win in the marketplace requires the commitment, cooperation, and participation of all four key links in produce chain: farmworkers, growers, retailers and consumers.

Exploring an Unprecedented Idea

In 2008, behind the leadership and vision of Costco Wholesale, an American multinational corporation which operates a chain of membership-only warehouse clubs, United Farm Workers, a labor union for farmworkers in the United States, and Oxfam America, a confederation of 20 independent charitable organizations, came together to explore an unconventional idea:

Could diverse interests across the produce industry align in new ways to offer greater assurance of fair working conditions for farmworkers and increased food safety?

Over the next three years, this question was thoroughly explored by representatives from each of the interest groups, bringing their organization's values and agenda forward.

This level of collaboration was unprecedented in the produce industry, and by providing equal voice to each stakeholder group, they arrived at a common purpose and certain core principles:

Purpose: *to protect farmworkers, consumers and the long-term viability of the fresh produce industry.*

Core Principles: *Continuous improvement, inclusion of the worker' voice, and rigorous standards developed through multi-stakeholder participation.*

The Equitable Food Initiative

Between 2011 and 2014, a pilot group of four Costco produce suppliers agreed to test the concept. These first four operations were certified, after successfully adapting the labor, food safety, and pest management standards through workforce development training and worker verification of compliance.

Having proved the concept, participating stakeholders agreed to launch an independent nonprofit enterprise in 2015, specifically for continuing and expanding this endeavor: The Equitable Food Initiative. *The EFI Mission: We bring together growers, farmworkers, retailers, and consumers to transform agriculture and improve the lives of farmworkers.*

Clarity of Purpose

With our mission agreed, representatives from each of the four interest groups identified the benefits they hoped to achieve through collaboration and cooperation.

FARMWORKERS BENEFIT	GROWERS BENEFIT	RETAILERS BENEFIT	CONSUMERS BENEFIT
Premium bonuses paid by retailers. Working conditions improved. Professional training and growth opportunities developed. Respectful, safe and harassment free	Recruitment challenges reduced & retention rates increased. Workforce collaboration for innovation and problem-solving attained. Communications and work	Food safety protocols and respectful working conditions assured. Consumer demand for socially responsible business practices met. Socially responsible	Risk of foodborne illness reduced. Values-based purchasing offered by easily identifiable responsible retailers.

FARMWORKERS BENEFIT	GROWERS BENEFIT	RETAILERS BENEFIT	CONSUMERS BENEFIT
workplaces ensured.	processes streamlined. Ambitious new on-farm standards and practices consistently and enduringly executed.	vendors screened and identified. Produce protected from contamination, risks reduced for recalls and foodborne illness.	

These criteria serve as ongoing measures of success for the Equitable Food Initiative.

Challenges

Expanding this initiative beyond four pilot sites generated honest skepticism among the stakeholders. Could EFI or any well-intentioned organization actually create labor/management teams on the farms and train farm workers to engage in continuous improvement efforts?

This skepticism was grounded in the long history of the traditional command and control management structure prevalent throughout agriculture. It was hard for many to imagine a setting where seasonal farmworkers would actively engage with their supervisors in problem solving and identifying and implementing improvement ideas. The supervisors were brains and the farmworkers were the brawn.

Adding to the skepticism is the fact that most farmworkers have limited formal education, making reading and writing additional challenges (median highest grade of school completed is sixth grade), 53% are undocumented (without legal authorization to be in the country), and are seasonal employees often moving between farms, crops and housing.[60]

Training Required

In order to overcome these challenges and build confidence in our approach, the need for training was obvious. Our group identified specific training to enable both farm supervisors and farm workers to more effectively work together. Initially we began with training designed to establish trust and collaboration. We then focused on innovative thinking required for problem solving and continuous improvement opportunities.

The proposal was to begin by training front-line workers and supervisors to prepare them to work together to ensure compliance with the labor, food safety, and pest management standards. This formula, in addition to broadening compliance responsibility, would improve quality and business results, foster employee engagement and uncover improvement opportunities.

Continuous Improvement in Action

A Continuous Improvement team in California went to work on improving the picking, packing, and distribution of strawberries to the largest retailers in the country. When a semi-truck load of produce is delivered from the farm to the retailer distribution center, it goes through testing for quality, stress (determines shelf life), and food safety. Samples are taken from each semi-truck and tested. If any of these criteria do not meet the retailer's standards, the entire truckload is rejected. A

60   SAF - Student Action with Farmworkers. United States Farmworker Factsheet. August, 2020. https://saf-unite.org/content/united-states-farmworker-factshee

semi-load of strawberries is estimated to be worth about $40,000.

On this farm, an average of 3-4 trucks a month were rejected. The Continuous Improvement Team needed to apply a comprehensive problem-solving strategy in addressing this issue. Since their initial perspective was limited to that of field work and the fruit cooler only. More data was needed to conduct a comprehensive root-cause analysis. To collect this data, the CI team now moved on to observe the harvesting of the fruit, loading onto field trucks, unloading into the field cooler, and the loading of the berries onto the semi-truck that would deliver the fruit to the retailers' distribution center the next day.

The CI team was next invited to tour the distribution center. Upon arrival, the retailer provided the group an overview of how they determine if produce meets their quality, shelf life, and food safety requirements. Next, they observed their berries being off-loaded and sample testing taking place. During the whole-time, team members were taking notes and questioning each step in the process. Team members also gained first-hand experience as they were allowed to personally test the berries using a thermostat. The Quality Control manager, at the Center, explained that, through this testing, she could determine if the berries were heat-stressed prior to being cooled which would directly impact quality shelf life. This new awareness, among CI team members, generated rousing discussions during the rest of the tour.

The following morning, the CI team met, compiled, and organized the data they had collected, analyzing each step in the process. Now, with a more complete understanding, the Team recognized that the long-held tradition of those in the field taking breaks and eating lunch at the same time contributed to the likelihood of berries becoming heat-stressed.

The retailer provides the CI Team an overview of how they determine if produce meets their quality, shelf life and food safety requirements.

The CI Team recommended the following solution: Stagger breaks so there is someone always available to drive the truck with berries to the cooler and someone available to assist in unloading at the cooler. By doing so, when the breaks were completed, there was always an empty truck with new boxes awaiting.

After the successful implementation of the staggered breaks, the CI Team then recommended adding an additional truck crew so there was continual picking, packing and ongoing quality assurance in the field. This change further improved quality and productivity as workers, being paid piece rate, did not need to rush to get their berries quality assured, recorded, and loaded. There was always an empty truck to fill.

Impact on the Problem: As a result of this singular CI initiative, within six weeks of implementation, zero trucks were rejected at the retailer. Company savings averaged $120,000-$130,000 per month.

Positive Outcomes Verified

In 2017-2018, BSD Consulting initiated a two-year study assessing the impact of the EFI initiative. BSD conducted 19 farm visits, held 21 Focus Groups, analyzed 81 Audit Reports and conducted 476 interviews. Their study found that "the EFI model is improving working conditions, developing skills in workers and managers, strengthening management systems, enhancing business performance and ultimately creating a culture shift within grower organizations."[61]

In the words of Shawn Hartley, owner and Vice-President at Onions 52: "EFI has helped us maximize our efficiencies in all aspects of our program and work areas. The EFI model gave workers a voice and a way to share their ideas and helped us work together to implement improvements, taking an efficient operation and making it even better."

Today there are 60 Equitable Food Initiative-certified locations, with more than 50,000 workers on farms with EFI teams and over $10 million paid in worker's bonuses.

---

61 BSD Consulting . "EFI's Worker Engagement Model Creates Positive Outcomes for Growers." November, 2019. https://equitablefood.org/latest-news/two-year-study-quantifies-equitable-food-initiative-program-effectiveness/

Looking To The Future

Continuous Improvement has been an integral part of the Equitable Food Initiative's efforts since its inception. Committing to continually improve encourages everyone in the produce chain to make progress. Training that is provided fosters trust and collaboration enabling stakeholders to engage in the constant monitoring of health and safety, labor, pest management, and food safety issues and to provide the innovative thinking required for continuous improvement.

What I have learned by working with the men and women that plant, grow, harvest, and deliver fresh produce to our tables is that perceived obstacles such as very diverse interest groups, untried ideas, workplace hierarchies, the lack of formal education, unpredictable legal status, and engaging temporary seasonal workers are not barriers at all, but actually "improvement opportunities" waiting for committed and creative Continuous Improvement Leaders to harvest.

Focus on Vision and Goals

MARCOS PAVANI
CDI Brazil

Improvement initiatives, business environments, and even human societies are actually living organisms full of interconnected systems. The overall health of the organism depends on the interdependence of these systems. If a system fails, it overloads or even damages the functioning of the whole.

For example, an ailing heart may not be able to maintain blood flow properly. This condition can overload the respiratory system and increase internal fluids pressure in the body creating a downward health spiral.

I make this small introduction in order to share part of my lifelong learnings of the implementation of continuous improvement initiatives.

My Early Days

In 1996, I was working for a large, multinational company in Brazil. Having recently transferred from the agribusiness division, I became the manufacturing manager of the Home Care Products Unit. At that time, we began to implement improvement systems based on Japanese philosophies and Total Productive Maintenance (TPM).

These new improvement techniques were completely unknown in our company. The work practices being introduced were very disciplined and rigorous. As a result, many in our organization found these methods frustrating and paralyzing.

Operators, supervisors, and managers all had difficulty understanding the importance of:

▶ Avoiding small variations in the production flow, which was a leading cause of quality issues when we failed to follow a precise production pattern.

▶ The influence of small flaws that can generate big losses. Example: tiny blemishes on finished products resulting in rejects.

▶ Output Variables: Long leadtime, unreasonable production schedule, high inventory rate, supply chain interruption.

▶ Cost Improvements: Low efficiency, idle people or machines, reducing scrap and energy losses.

▶ The lack of discipline in standard work (colleagues deviating from set manufacturing steps).

After all, site results and the overall results of the company had always been considered as the best in the market. Why should we change? Why should we improve what has already been recognized as great?

Lack of Understanding

The managerial pressure to adopt new methods and systems did not allow us to lay the proper foundation. The opportunity to explain to our team members the purpose and objectives of our new ways of working was missed. We were focused on improving results quickly.

Our Japanese consultants contributed to this disconnect by focusing entirely on *What we should do, but never Why we should do it.*

Over the next two years, each area at our site implemented new practices following a rigorous agenda. Production efficiencies showed impressive improvements with "world class" results. Material losses were reduced to less than 1/3 of the original values, safety incidents dropped, and quality indicators improved dramatically.

Celebrating Success

We had achieved many accomplishments! The motivation and energy in the work environment was palpable! The team that coordinated the implementation of the new system was now prepared for the final audits, and recognition of the program's success.

In October 1998, the plant was audited by our Japanese mentors and in November recognized for having won the Excellence Award! Quite an achievement! Joy was everywhere. Being part of that success was really a great moment for the entire workforce.

New Challenges

However, the business world does not give you much time to celebrate. Planning to meet new requirements in the immediate future was necessary. The revision of the ISO 9000 Standards (standards that helps ensure organizations meet statutory and regulatory requirements related to a product or service) was already on the agenda and very urgent. The team quickly went back to work to implement these new standards.

Finally, after achieving our latest ISO goals, we reassessed our award-winning improvement process. We immediately recognized that we had lost much of what had been achieved. Some of the best efficiencies were no longer satisfactory. Quality problems and product losses that were under control were now re-occurring.

What Went Wrong?

In order to comply with the new ISO standards, changes in our newly refined work processes were ordered. Deadlines dictated our decisions, and we quickly implemented the necessary requirements – as a result, our teams and processes suffered.

Some of our findings included:

▶ Thanks to the introduction of TPM and focusing each day on improving throughput and quality, the Overall Equipment Effectiveness (OEE) improved from a rate of 82% to average 92%. As the focus shifted to meeting the ISO 9000 Standards, OEE fell back to 85% - a huge productivity loss.

▶ Daily front-line team meetings had boasted an attendance rate of 100% and generated hundreds of improvement initiatives. As the focus shifted to ISO 9000 attainment, participation in daily meeting dropped by 50% Now, half of team members were devoting more time to the new ISO program and less to solving normal operating challenges. As a result, teams experienced resurgence in quality issues and losses in productivity.

▶ Safety accidents also spiked coinciding with the losses in OEE. As productivity decreased, more "hands on machines" were required. These manual adjustments unfortunately resulted in more hand and arm injuries.

Our leadership team rallied together to understand what had gone wrong and create a plan of action to prevent backsliding in the future. We determined that our leadership team had been focused primarily on accomplishing the immediate requirement – the flavor of the month. We had been results-focused and were proud to hit our targets.

What We Learned

We leaders realized that we had drifted from the vision and long-term goals of our organization. When a new priority was announced, the regimens required in sustaining past accomplishments were abandoned. We eagerly jumped in to tackle the latest challenge. *We incorrectly believed that improvements would be self-sustaining, that people would be able to stay focused on all fronts – AND WE WERE WRONG.*

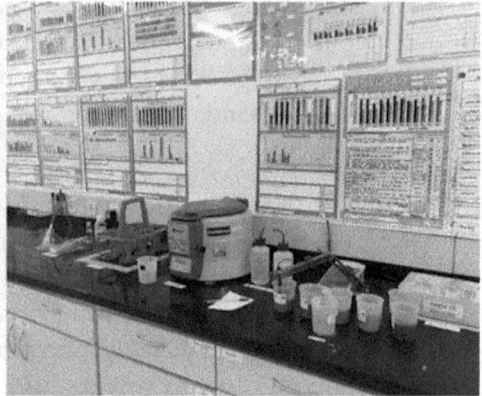

Beware of the "flavor of the month." Never lose site of the long-term Vision and Goals of your organization.

In our quest to "hit our numbers," we had forgotten the "Purpose" and "Why" we were in pursuit of improving systems. Thus, we were creating a culture that was excellent at achieving the current priorities, but failing to sustain and nurture the behaviors and best practices necessary for the long term.

Lessons to share: *the importance of maintaining a laser-like focus on the vision and long-term goals of the organization. When too much attention is focused on one initiative, others often suffer. Keeping this perspective will lessen the urge to chase the flavor of the month and channel energies on the big picture.*

SECTION 5
LEARN AND LEAD

SOLUTIONS TECHNOLOHY

SCIENCE INNOVATION

SKILLS WISDOM

SYSTEM

PRACTICE LEADERSHIP COMPETENCE

LEARN AND LEAD

EXPERIENCE CONTINUOS

PROCESSES

STRATEGY IMPROVEMENTS

Continuous Learning for Continuous Improvement Leaders

"Your vehicle of leadership is fueled by your willingness to learn. You can't lead if you can't learn!"

Israelmore Ayivor,
Author and Inspirational Writer

Keeping Pace With Change

The ever-accelerating pace and significance of technological change can be destabilizing. Even as we write this chapter, we recognize that statistics we quote and projections experts make are likely obsolete even as the ink dries.

What is occurring is historically unprecedented and will ultimately affect all types of organizations and their members here and around the world.

Most CEOs (90 percent) believe their company is facing disruptive change driven by digital technologies, and 70 percent say their organization does not have the skills to adapt. This doubt reflects the fact that skills are becoming outmoded at an accelerating rate. Software engineering for example, is a dynamic field that requires continuous learning and adaptation to new technologies, programming languages, frameworks, and best practices.[62] Professionals in marketing, sales, manufacturing, law, accounting, and finance report similar demands.

---

[62] Forbes

Our challenge, as CI leaders, is to anticipate and exploit technological advances in ways that enable our organizations to thrive and grow.

To appreciate the scope and speed at which technological change is occurring, just look at a few that are reshaping our lives.

▶ The Internet and Digital Age

▶ Human Knowledge

▶ The Internet of Things (IoT)

▶ Artificial Intelligence (AI)

"The pace of change and the threat of disruption creates tremendous opportunities."

Steve Case - CEO Revolution LLC

The Internet and Digital Age

The **Internet** is a global system of interconnected computer networks that uses the Internet protocol suite to communicate between networks and devices. It is a network of networks that consists of private, public, academic, business and government networks of local to global scope, linked by a broad array of electronic, wireless and optical networking technologies.

The Internet carries a vast range of information resources and services, such as the interlinked hypertext documents and applications of the World Wide Web (WWW), electronic mail, telephony and file sharing. *Wikipedia*

In October 2023, of the 8.1 billion people in the world, approximately 5.3 billion people had Internet access! This equates to 65.7 percent of the global population. Of this total, 4.95 billion, or 61.4 percent of the world's population, were social medial users. 63

The impact of over two-thirds of the total global population having access to instant communications and boundless information is triggering momentous changes that will continue throughout our lifetimes. Although this technology is not evenly distributed, the same benefits and challenges extend to every corner of the globe.

Even in remote environments, people have access to the Internet through personal computers, phones, or other mobile devices. This access dramatically increases the utilization and impact of the Internet throughout the developing world.

Global Internet Usage

Connecting billions of people worldwide, the Internet is a core pillar of the modern information society. Northern Europe ranked first among worldwide regions by the share of the population using the Internet in 2023. In Norway, Saudi Arabia, and the United Arab Emirates, 99 percent of the population used the Internet as of April 2023. North Korea was at the opposite end of the spectrum, with virtually no Internet usage penetration among the general population, ranking last worldwide.

The Digital Age

The Digital or Information Age, as it is also known, is this historical period in which we have been living since the mid-20th century. This era has been marked by a gradual shift from traditional heavy manufacturing industries such as steel making, farm machinery, textiles, auto production etc., to service and technology industries like health, finance, engineering, recreation,

---

[63] STATISTA

custodial services and computers. [64] This move to the Digital Age was enabled by the widespread use of digital logic, transistors, integrated circuit chips and their derived technologies including computers, microprocessors, digital cellular phones and the Internet. These technological innovations have transformed traditional production and business techniques. [65]

Countries with the largest digital populations in the world as of January 2023

(in millions) *Statista*

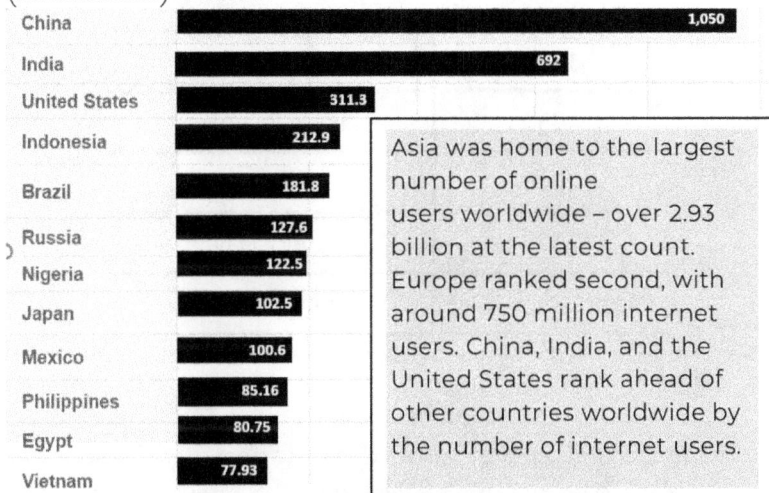

Country	Millions
China	1,050
India	692
United States	311.3
Indonesia	212.9
Brazil	181.8
Russia	127.6
Nigeria	122.5
Japan	102.5
Mexico	100.6
Philippines	85.16
Egypt	80.75
Vietnam	77.93

Asia was home to the largest number of online users worldwide – over 2.93 billion at the latest count. Europe ranked second, with around 750 million internet users. China, India, and the United States rank ahead of other countries worldwide by the number of internet users.

Human Knowledge "Explosion"

Along with this seismic shift from the Industrial Era to the Digital Age, another technological tsunami was occurring thanks to the expansion and sharing of human knowledge. In 1982, futurist and inventor Buckminster Fuller created "The Knowledge Doubling Curve." Fuller estimated that until 1900, human knowledge doubled approximately every 100 years. Since then, every decade

---

[64] Encyclopedia.com

[65] Wikipedia

has eclipsed that growth rate. By 1950, the human knowledge rate was doubling approximately every 25 years! 66

Digital Age Hastens Knowledge Sharing

Dr. Tim Sandle, science writer and journalist, at Science/AAAS explained, "Since the end of World War II thanks to the advance of new technologies, improved communications and the dawn of the Digital Age, knowledge development and sharing, throughout the world, broadly expanded." Recognizing that different types of knowledge have dissimilar rates of growth, Sandle presented the following **doubling of knowledge estimates**:

1900	Every 100 years
1950	Every 25 years
2000	Every year
2020	Every Day
Predicted by IBM*	Every 12 hours

* the build out of the "Internet of Things" will lead to the doubling of knowledge every 12 hours!

How this colossal burst of knowledge will affect organizations and society is yet to be determined; however, this rapid expansion and sharing of knowledge through the Internet offers a potential to solve many of today's challenges and mysteries.

---

66 Buckminster

The Internet of Things (IoT)

The Internet of Things (IoT) refers to a network of physical devices, vehicles, appliances and other physical objects that are embedded with sensors, software and network connectivity that allows them to collect and share data. These devices – also known as "smart objects" – can range from simple "smart home" devices like smart thermostats, to wearables like smartwatches and RFID-enabled clothing, to complex industrial machinery and transportation systems. *IBM*

Add the Internet of Things (IoT) to our new reality. The IoT refers to all the devices that connect to the Internet and/or other devices. For example, your computer, smartphone, vehicle, coffee pot, optic doorbell, wearables, almost anything you can imagine can, through a WI-FI connection, be linked in a way that provides data and contributes to human knowledge.

For example, Google Maps and Waze, popular navigation apps, collect information such as construction areas, congestion, collision and speed traps from commuters using these apps or their vehicle GPS (Global Positioning System) as they drive. This information is then instantly conveyed to other commuters who may not have departed yet for their destination.

"IoT is an emerging technology that is on the path of rapid developmental growth. Automobiles, goods and services, sensors, consumer durables and industry and utility components, among others, are now aligned with the Internet and data analytic capabilities, which is transforming the way people work, live and think." Projections are: "more than 100 billion IoT connected devices will be installed by 2025, generating a revenue close to $10 trillion." [67]

---

67   Laura Wood. "Global Sensors in Internet of Things (IoT) Devices Market, Analysis & Forecast: 2016 to 2022; (Focus on Pressure, Temperature, Light, Chemical, & Motion Sensors; and

Matthew Evans, the IoT program head at techUK, explained in a WIRED article by Matt Burgess: "By combining these connected devices with automated systems, it is possible to gather information, analyze it and create an action to help someone with a particular task, or learn from a process. IoT offers us opportunity to be more efficient in how we do things, saving us time, money and often emissions in the process; it allows companies, governments and public authorities to re-think how they deliver services and produce goods." [68]

Artificial Intelligence – The Age of AI

> **Artificial Intelligence (AI)** is a field of computer science that focuses on creating machines that can perform tasks that would typically require human intelligence. AI encompasses a wide range of techniques and approaches, but at its core, it involves creating algorithms and models that enable machines to learn from data, reason and make decisions. Britannica

(Description of Artificial Intelligence and potential uses listed below are a compilation from various AI providers and sources. Because this application of computer science is new and constantly evolving, accurate predictions of its use and impact are yet to be uncovered.)

Applications in Healthcare, Manufacturing, Retail & Transportation). Business Wire. March, 2017. https://www.businesswire.com/news/home/20170302005653/en/Global-Sensors-IoT-Devices-Market-Grow-26.91

[68] Matt Burgess. "What is the Internet of Things? *WIRED*. February 16, 2018.

THE PROS

AI can be used to solve problems, make predictions, and automate tasks. This rapidly growing field has the potential to revolutionize the way we live and work [69].

Developers claim that AI can be used in many diverse fields such as healthcare, finance, manufacturing, transportation, agriculture and many others.

For example:

▶ **Healthcare:** Research, administration and training, public health, diagnose diseases and develop personalized treatment plans, reduce surgeries, patient engagement, remote medicine, hospital care.

▶ **Finance:** Detect fraud, manage risks, make investment decisions, debt collection, regulatory compliance, customer service.

▶ **Manufacturing:** Assist manufactures with predictive maintenance, generative design, price forecasting, quality control, robotics, supply chain optimization, inventory management, research and development.

▶ **Transportation:** Optimize traffic flow, improve safety, lessen carbon emissions, delivery predictions, self-driving vehicles.

▶ **Agriculture:** Predict supply chain behavior and customer demand, identifying macro weather patterns, crop monitoring, , auto weeding and harvesting, yield mapping and prediction, tracking: soil, crop and animal health.

---

[69] Forbes

THE CONS

While AI presents great opportunities, there are also several consequences and concerns associated with AI. For example:

- ▶ **Job losses**: AI can replace human workers in many tasks, especially those that are repetitive, routine, or low-skill.

- ▶ **Bias caused by bad data**: AI systems rely on data to learn and make decisions, but if the data is incomplete, inaccurate, or biased, the AI outputs can also be flawed or discriminatory.

- ▶ **Privacy violations**: AI can collect, analyze, and use large amounts of personal data, such as online behavior, location, health, or biometrics.

- ▶ **Lack of human-like creativity and empathy**: AI can perform well on tasks that have clear rules and objectives, but it may struggle with tasks that require creativity, imagination, or emotional intelligence.

- ▶ **Uncontrollable self-aware AI**: AI can potentially become self-aware, autonomous, and super-intelligent, surpassing human intelligence and capabilities.

Despite these concerns, AI appears to have the potential to bring about many benefits in the next decade. However, it is important to ensure that the development of AI is done in an ethical and responsible manner.[70]

How Can We Prepare?

These amazing technological advances are presently reshaping our world. It is impossible to predict the specific changes that new technologies will generate in your industry and organization.

---

[70] forbes.com2. rockcontent.com3. tableau.com

However, as experienced CI leaders, we know what we must do to prepare:

- ▶ Accept that change is certain and that every organization and industry is affected.

- ▶ Recognize that the impact of technology is often unpredictable.

- ▶ Constantly update our skills and knowledge.

- ▶ Assist our organizations in understanding and adapting to changes.

- ▶ Prepare and equip ourselves by adopting a continuous-learning lifestyle.

Continuous Learning Versus Traditional Learning

Corporations and organizations have been providing learning opportunities to employees for decades. Many organizations provide stipends or tuition rebates to staff who take courses aligned with their employment. For the employee and the employer, it makes sense.

But there is a big difference between taking a course and making a commitment to continuous learning. The motivation to take job-related classes is typically tied to promotional opportunities or a new job, whereas continuous learning is a more personal philosophy about our approach to work and life.

Continuous Learning is the relentless pursuit of seeking out new information and expanding our skill-set through education, training, study, experience, following industry trends, identifying best practice, sharing knowledge, work-related networking, case studies, blog postings, podcasts, social media, etc.

Throughout our working lives, as advocates for continuous improvement, **we are required to look ahead** and seek out and identify changes occurring both near and far that offer improvement opportunities to our organizations.

With the same focus and commitment that we introduce new methods and skills in our organizations, we must apply a similar approach to enhancing our individual learning and competencies. In order to remain relevant and valued members, CI Leaders must continually generate incremental improvements in ourselves that translate into a competitive advantage for our organization. Relentlessly pursuing new information and expanding our skills models the behavior we are seeking in others and is consistent with our continuous improvement beliefs and aspirations.

Continuous Improvement Depends on Us

Throughout our CI careers, the demand to constantly acquire new knowledge and skills is never-ending. This commitment to continuous learning requires self-motivation and a hunger to uncover and implement new ideas – to push the boundaries. It requires a singular commitment to constantly be on the lookout for changes in methods, skills, technology, research, tools, education and training. Now, as ever, there is always more to know and learn.

> There was a time we felt badly saying: "If we had known last year, what we now know, we could have been more helpful to our clients." Recently we concluded that *when we can no longer make that claim, we will have stopped learning*.

"The capacity to learn is a gift; the ability to learn is a skill; the willingness to learn is a choice."

Brian Herbert

FINAL THOUGHTS

"An organization, no matter how well designed, is only as good as the people who live and work in it."

Dee Ward Hock,
founder of Visa credit card association

We began this book by presenting the dilemma that we faced in working with two, seemingly identical work sites, that experienced <u>very different</u> outcomes. Solving this "puzzle" was the impetus for this book with the goal to provide CI leaders with a greater understanding of the keys necessary to create a successful and sustainable culture of improvement. To this end, we shared the lessons we have learned through education, experience, trial and error, advice from others and perseverance.

In the "Roots" chapter, we presented certain aspects of organizational change that are fundamental to successful change efforts. We see these building blocks as complementary to what you already know, may have learned through your experiences and/or can be added to your knowledge base. The "Roots" content may seem elementary or inconsequential, yet we have found them vital to the understanding of "change" that every CI leader should grasp.

The "Five Keys" chapter identifies the vital factors that make the difference between success and failure in continuous improvement initiatives. In this introduction to the key principles, we show how to establish each of the factors and nurture the most essential element of successful improvement initiatives: **the people.**

In the "Fixes" chapter, we provide useful tools to address everyday challenges and guidance for resolving common issues you will face. Those of us engaged in this type of work encounter resistance and setbacks of all types, and having an arsenal of potential corrective actions, can take some of the bumps out of the road.

The next section is called "Share Your Story." We enlisted five well respected colleagues, who have worked in very different situations, to share consequential lessons learned.

Lastly, we take a glimpse as to how technology is reshaping our world faster in more ways than in any time in human history. This volatility will impact your organization. The need for continuous improvement will only increase as organizations grapple with increasing global competition and the introduction of technological advances.

The One Constant

As unsettling as it may be to know change is coming at us faster and more unpredictably from all directions, we can take heart in knowing that the lessons contained in this book will hold true.

While new technologies and business initiatives will remain volatile and continually impact our organizations, The Five Keys presented in this book are proven attributes for successfully dealing with each new challenge. The work of leaders, engagement of colleagues, alignment around goals, member accountability and the resources to get the job done are the same requisite elements found in successful organizations throughout history. And each of these elements has a direct and consequential impact on the human equation.

We live in a time when the value and impact of "the people in organizations" is often discounted and taken for granted. Many have come to believe that success awaits in the latest new technology, new products, new tools, new system, new anything, forgetting that the successful adoption and application of each new "breakthrough" depends on the human element, how it is adopted and applied.

Regardless of the type of organization in which you are leading CI efforts - service, manufacturing, merchandizing, technology, medical, government, union, non-profit, etc. - and regardless of the challenges that your organization faces, the common denominator to successfully meeting these challenges will continue to be the human factor.

You and your colleagues will always be the essential players who convert strategy to actions and deliver value to your stakeholders. *The people in your organization are the primary catalysts of success.*

BIBLIOGRAPHY

2014, Deloitte - Global Human Capital Trends. 2014. Engaging the 21st Century Workforce. Accessed July 11, 2020. https://www2.deloitte.com/content/dam/Deloitte/ar/Documents/human-capital/arg_hc_global-human-capital-trends-2014_09062014%20(1).pdf.

Andrew Robertson, Nate Dvorak, Jennifer Robinson. 2019. Five Ways to Promote Accountability. June 19. Accessed September 23, 2019. https://www.gallup.com/workplace/257945/ways-create-company-culture-accountability.aspx.

Associates, Dannemiller Tyson. 2000. Whole-Scale Change - Unleashing the Magic in Organizations. San Francisco: Berrett - Koehler.

Atkinson, Gary Devlin - Phil. 2017. The Benefits of a Culture of Trust. January. Accessed July 22, 2020. https://www.scott-moncrieff.com/assets/publications/The_Benefits_of_a_Culture_of_Trust_-_a_report_by_Scott-Moncrieff.pdf.

Aurik, Martijn. 2017. Businesses waste $37 billion on ineffective meetings every year. What's your share? July 13. Accessed May 10, 2020. https://www.getminute.com/ineffective-meetings/.

Bill Pelster, Dani Johnson, Jen Temple, Benard van der Vyver. 2017. Careers and Learning: Real Time, All the Time. February 28. Accessed August 10, 2019. https://www2.deloitte.com/us/en/insights/focus/human-capital-trends/2017/learning-in-the-digital-age.html.

Bukminster, Fuller R. 1981. *Critical Path*. New York: St. Martin's Press.

Burgess, Matt. 2018. What is the Internet of Things. February
16. Accessed February 1, 2020.
https://www.wired.co.uk/article/internet-of-things-
what-is-explained-iot.

CBC News. Archived from the original on June 9, 2007.
Retrieved May 29, 2007. n.d. CBC News. Archived from
the original on June 9, 2007. Retrieved May 29, 2007.

Chakarova, Vessela and others. 2013. Federal Reserve History.
November 22. Accessed 2020.
https://www.federalreservehistory.org/essays/oil_shoc
k_of_1978_79.

Clement, J. 2020. Statista. June 4. Accessed July 22, 2020.
https://www.statista.com/statistics/617136/digital-
population-worldwide/.

Congress, American Experience - Library of. n.d. The Rise of
American Consumerism. Accessed November 2019.
pbs.org/value.

Crabtree, Steve. 2013. Gallup - World. October 13. Accessed
June 10, 2017.
https://news.gallup.com/poll/165269/worldwide-
employees-engaged-work.aspx.

Dishman, Lydia. 2018. The complicated and troubled history
of the annual performance review. November 7.
Accessed August 28, 2020.
https://www.fastcompany.com/90260641/the-
complicated-and-troubled-history-of-the-annual-
performance-review.

Drucker, Peter. 2001. *The Essential Drucker*. New York: Harper
Business.

Equitable Food, 2019. EFI's Worker Engagement Model
Creates Positive Outcomes for Growers - Shippers.

November 12. Accessed September 2, 2020. https://equitablefood.org/latest-news/two-year-study-quantifies-equitable-food-initiative-program-effectiveness/.

"Farmworker Health Fact Sheet." NCFH Inc. . September. Accessed July 9, 2020. http://www.ncfh.org/uploads/3/8/6/8/38685499/fs-migrant_demographics.pdf.

Farmworkers, SAF - Student Action with. 2020. United States Farmworker Factsheet. August 27. Accessed August 27, 2020. https://saf-unite.org/content/united-states-farmworker-factsheet.

Fechtman, Dave. 2018. The Three Guiding Principles for Creating an Intentional Culture. January 26. Accessed September 29, 2020. https://www.forbes.com/sites/forbescoachescouncil/2018/01/26/the-three-guiding-principles-for-creating-an-intentional-culture/.

Foster, Carrie. 2012. Organization Development. September 10. Accessed July 4, 2020. http://organisationdevelopment.org/the-theorists-richard-beckhard/.

Gillis, Mergy, Shalleck. 2013. Beliefs, Behaviors & Results - The Chief Executive's Guide to Delivering Superior Shareholder Value. Austin, TX: Greenleaf Book Group Press.

Grand View Research. 2018. Market Analysis Report. U.S. Fruit & Vegetable Market Size, Share and Trends Analysis Report, San Francisco: same.

____. 2018. U.S. Fruit & Vegetables Market Zize and Trends Analysis Report. Market Analysis Report, San Francisco: Grand View Research.

Hammer, James A. Champy & Michael M. 1993. *Reengineering the Corporation*. New York: Harper Collins - Business.

Hanke, Stacey. 2018. Three Steps to Overcoming Resistance. August 14. Accessed July 29, 2020. https://www.forbes.com/sites/forbescoachescouncil/2018/08/14/three-steps-to-overcoming-resistance/#7b97ec485eae.

Harter, Jim. 2018. Employee Engagement on the Rise in U.S. August 26. Accessed July 11, 2020. news.gallup.com/poll/241649employee-engagement-rise.aspx.

Haspel, Tamar. 2017. *Washington Post*. March 17. Accessed July 9, 2020. https://www.washingtonpost.com/lifestyle/food/in-an-immigration-crackdown-who-will-pick-our-produce/2017/03/17/.

Industry, Training. 2019. The Leadership Training Market. March 28. Accessed July 10, 2020. https://trainingindustry.com/wiki/leadership/the-leadership-training-market/.

Initiative, Equitable Food. 2020. Bringing Everyone to the Table to Transform Agriculture. Accessed July 10, 2020. https://equitablefood.org/.

2020. EFI Standards. Accessed July 11, 2020. https://equitablefood.org/efi-standards.

Institute, Stastic Brain Research. 2017. Startup Business Failure By Industry . May 5. Accessed July 10, 2020. https://www.statisticbrain.com/startup-failure-by-industry/.

International, Weight Watchers. 2017. 2016 Annual Report. Form 10K, Washington, DC: United States Securities and Exchnge Commission.

Jansen, Rudi. 2019. If you are too busy to build good systems you'll always be too busy. February 22. Accessed December 12, 2019. https://www.rudijansen.com/too-busy-to-build-good-systems/.

KaiNexus. 2020. The ROI of Continuous Improvement. Accessed July 10, 2020. https://www.kainexus.com/roi-of-continuous-improvement.

Kaplan, David P. Norton & Robert S. 1996. *The Balanced Scorecard.* Cambridge: Harvard Business Press.

Kathleen Stansberry, Janna Anderson, Lee Raine. 2019. The Internet Will Continue to Make Life Better. October 28. Accessed February 15, 2020. https://www.pewresearch.org/internet/2019/10/28/4-the-internet-will-continue-to-make-life-better/.

Kettell, Steven. 2007. *Encyclopedia Britannica.* https://www.britannica.com/topic/oil-crisis.

Kotter, John P. 2012. *Leading Change.* Brighton, MA: *Harvard Business Review Press.*

—. 2013. When CEOs Talk Strategy, 70% of the Company Doesn't Get It. July 9. Accessed November 12, 2018. https://www.forbes.com/sites/johnkotter/2013/07/09/heres-why-ceo-strategies-fall-on-deaf-ears/#1c1f85753663.

Koulopoulos, Thomas. 2018. INC. Performance Reviews are Dead. Here's what you should do instead . February 25. Accessed August 30, 2020. https://www.inc.com/thomas-koulopoulos/performance-reviews-are-dead-heres-what-you-should-do-instead.html.

Leith, Jack Martin. 2019. "70% of Organizational Change Initiatives Fail" Fact or Fiction. Accessed March 13, 2020. http://jackmartinleith.com/70-percent-change-failure-rate/.

Lewis, Josh. 2008. Big Three Auto CEO's Flew Private Jets to Ask for Taxpayers Money. November 19. Accessed April 11, 2019. https://www.cnn.com/2008/US/11/19/autos.ceo.jets/.

Lewis, Michael. 2003. *Moneyball: The Art of Winning an Unfair Game*. New York: W.W. Norton & Co.

Lovecraft, H.P. 1973. *Supernatural Horror in Literature*. Dover Publications. (Mineola, NY: Dover Publishing.)

Mann, Ben Wigert and Annamarie. 2017. Give Performance Reviews that actually inspire employees. September 25. Accessed August 28, 2020. https://www.gallup.com/workplace/236135/give-performance-reviews-actually-inspire-employees.asp.

Mann, David. 2005. *Creating a Lean Culture*. New York: Productivity Press.

Mauboussin, Michael J. 2012. The True Measures of Success. Oct. Accessed July 15, 2019. https://hbr.org/2012/10/the-true-measures-of-success.

Milestones 1969-1976 Oil Embargo, 1973–1974. n.d. Office of the Historian. https://history.state.gov/milestones/1969-1976/oil-embargo.

Moore, Jeff. 2019. 101 on Digital Tranformation: What is it & How is it Reshaping Business? . August 21. Accessed

July 10, 2020. https://www.bairesdev.com/blog/digital-transformation-reshaping-businesses.

Murray, W.H. 2002. *The Evidence of Things Not Seen: A Mountaineer's Tale.* London: Baton Wicks.

NCFH. 2018. "Farmworkers Health Fact Sheet." National Center for Farmworkers Health. April. Accessed July 9, 2020. http://www.ncfh.org/facts-about-agricultural-workers.html.

Neher, William. 1997. Organizational Communications: Challenges of Change, Diverscty and Continuity. Boston: Allyn & Bacon .

Payscale .com. 2018. Variable Pay Trends Into 2018: who gets it, what types and why. April 30. Accessed August 28, 2020. https://www.payscale.com/compensation-today/2018/04/variable-pay-trends#:~:text=While%20Individual%20performance%20is%20highly,team%20performance%20(40%20percent).

_____. 2017. Variable Pay: Is there a difference between a bonus and an incentive? June 30. Accessed August 28, 2020. http://www.payschle.com.compensation-today/2017/06/difference-bonus-incentive.

Rhee, Brian Ross & Joseph. 2008. Big Three CEO's Flew Private Jets to Plead for Public Funds. November 18. Accessed April 11, 2019. https://abcnews.go.com/Blotter/WallStreet/story?id=6 285739&page=1.

Rogers, Everett M. 1962. *Diffusion of Innovations.* New York: Free Press .

Rozo, Gleeson -. 2013. The Silo Mentality: How to Break Down the Barriers - *Forbes.* October 2. Accessed July 5, 2020.

https://www.forbes.com/sites/brentgleeson/2013/10/02 /the-silo-mentality-how-to-break-down-the- barriers/#49414b318c7e.

Sadove, Stephen, interview by Adam Bryant. 2010. Chief Executive - Saks, Inc. (May 2010).

Salsburg, David. n.d. Course Hero - Texas A&M Univesity. Accessed July 5, 2020. https://www.coursehero.com/file/prdt5a/David- Salsburg-wrote-He-was-known-for-his-kindness-to- and-consideration-for/.

Samuelson, William, and Richard Zeckhauser. 1988 . "Status Quo Bias in Decision Making." Journal of Risk and Uncertainty vol. 1, no. 1, pp. 7-59.

Schein, Edgar H. 1985. *Organizational Culture and Leadership.* San Francisco: Josey-Bass.

Scott, Ryan. 2017. *Forbes.* June 1. Accessed January 15, 2019. https://www.forbes.com/sites/causeintegration/2017/0 6/01/employee-engagement-is-declining- worldwide/#2a0f15eb34e2.

Smither, James W., and Manuel London. 2009. Performance Management: putting research into action. San Francisco: Josey-Bass.

Sorenson, Susan. 2013. How Employee Engagement Drives Growth. June 20. Accessed July 11, 2020. gallup.com/workplace/236927/employee - engagement - drives - growth.aspx.

Stephanie Farquhar, PhD,corresponding author Nargess Shadbeh, JD, Julie Samples, JD, Santiago Ventura, BS, and Nancy Goff, BS. n.d. "Occupational Conditions and Well-Being of Indigenous Farmworkers." PMC.

Tasler, Nick. 2017. Stop Using the Excuse 'Organizational Change is Hard' . July 19. Accessed June 10, 2019. https://hbr.org/2017/07/stop-using-the-excuse-organizational-change-is-hard.

Tavis, Peter Cappelli and Anna. 2016. The Performance Management Revolution. October. Accessed August 30, 2020. https://hbr.org/2016/10/the-performance-management-revolution.

The Business Dictionary. http://www.businessdictionary.com/definition/silo-mentality.html.

Tutt, Andrew. 2019. Imagining the Internet - A History and Forcast. October 28. Accessed Februaary 15, 2020. https://www.elon.edu/u/imagining/surveys/x-2-internet-50th-2019.

U.S. Bureau of Labor Statistics. 2019. Retail Sales Workers. Washington: U.S. Government.

_____. 2020. Retail Sales Workers. Occupational Outlook Handbook, Washington: U.S. Government.

U.S. Fruit & Vegetable Market Size, Share, Industry Report 2018-2025. Analysis, San Francisco: Grand View Research. 2018

Vinney, Cynthia. 2019. Status Quo Bias: What it Means and How it Affect Your Behavior. December 11. Accessed July 11, 2020. thoughtco.com/status-quo-bias-4172981.

Vlasic, Bill. 2009. Choosing Its Own Path, Ford Stayed Independant . April 8. Accessed May 6, 2019. https://www.nytimes.com/2009/04/09/business/09ford.html.

Web-Japan, Ministry of Foreign Affairs, Japan. n.d. Japanese Economy Ater World War II. Accessed 2019.

http://factsanddetails.com/japan/cat24/sub155/item28
00.html#chapter-3.

Wickens, Peter. 1995. *The Ascendant Organization*. London:
Palgrave MacMillian.

Wood, Laura. 2017. Global Sensors in IoT Devices Market to
Grow 26.91% by 2022 - IoT Connected Devices to
Generate a Revenue of $10 Trillion - Research and
Markets. March 2. Accessed January 11, 2020.
https://www.businesswire.com/news/home/20170302
005653/en/Global-Sensors-IoT-Devices-Market-Grow-
26.91.

www.ingramcontent.com/pod-product-compliance
Lightning Source LLC
Chambersburg PA
CBHW070343090426
42733CB00009B/1265